José

GOD
FOUND ME
IN LOS ANGELES

JOSÉ VICENTE ROJAS

REVIEW AND HERALD® PUBLISHING ASSOCIATION
HAGERSTOWN, MD 21740

The author assumes full responsibility for the accuracy of all facts and quotations as cited in this book.

This book was
Edited by Gerald Wheeler
Designed by Willie Duke
Cover photo by Joel D. Springer
Electronic make-up by Shirley M. Bolivar
Typeset: 11/23 Bembo

PRINTED IN U.S.A.

03 02 01 00 99   5 4 3 2 1

R&H Cataloging Service
Rojas, José Vicente, 1960-
    José: God found me in Los Angeles

    1. Rojas, José Vicente, 1960-
I. Title

[B]

ISBN 0-8280-1438-8

Dedication

To my parents,

Luis Trejo and Juana Estela Rojas,

who overcame overwhelming

physical and emotional odds to give me an

opportunity for a life with Christ.

ACKNOWLEDGMENTS

This book, like many others, is the result of countless hours of prayer, reflection, and work, with the support of key people. My wife, Ruthie, and my children, Veronica, Angelica, and Gabriel, inspired me to write freely and honestly about our lives. My prayer partner, Patrick Kenny, helped me to keep focused on the spiritual goals for leadership reflected in this volume. And, because of her belief in me, my administrative assistant, Judy Winkle, encouraged me consistently until the manuscript was complete.

CHAPTER ONE

"MAMÁ, WHAT'S WRONG WITH ME?"

The palm trees gently swayed in the cool breeze that Saturday morning I made my unexpected entry into the world. It was March 26, 1960, and at 9:00 a.m. the County General Hospital in East Los Angeles swarmed with its usual hectic activity. Patients, medical personnel, and others crowded the hallways as if everyone had waited until that precise moment to rush to the hospital. My mom had had a long night in the delivery suite, with her most difficult moment occurring that morning at 8:01 when I was born. She now rested quietly in her room while I was lying bundled up in a soft blanket, sleeping in my crib among the choir of about 15 crying babies from the previous night's deliveries.

When my dad arrived, he stood at the viewing window, seeking his first glimpse of the newest addition to the Rojas family. Although only 22, he and my mom already had two boys at home. Yet the moment was new and special for him because he had not been able to be present for the birth of my older brother, Louie, Jr. My oldest brother, Gerry, was my mom's son from a previous marriage. At the time of Louie's birth Dad had been working in Los Angeles while my mom remained in El Paso, Texas. He had been trying to earn enough money to bring Mom to live with him in L.A. Consequently, Louie was more than a month old before dad saw him for the first time.

As Dad stared at me inquisitively from the window, he marveled at my full head of hair, including a plentiful amount on my face, something that most people joke is still true today. When he spotted me, Dad erupted with a joyful noise that he probably meant as a giggle. His strange noises accompanied an assortment of funny facial expressions that must have puzzled anyone seeing him, but Dad enjoyed his first attempts at bonding. Then he went to see my mother. As he walked into her room, talking excitedly about his new son, he cheerfully kissed her. My mom could smell the alcohol on his breath.

Beginnings

Things were not good at home. My dad, Luis Trejo Rojas, had one of the strongest addictions to alcohol that I have ever encountered. A difficult childhood had apparently driven him to alcoholism as a way of escape. The abuse he suffered had affected him emotionally and had given a hard edge to his personality. Dad's drinking, an almost daily excursion into oblivion, left him constantly angry and often violent. Pain was a frequent presence in our home.

I had chosen that particular morning to be born because the night before my father had beaten my mom, causing her to go into labor. While the joy at having another child that day helped ease the previous night's abuse, it certainly didn't erase it. Her life was a classic example of the battered wife syndrome. Constantly hoping that we could have a happy home, she often asked God at Sunday Mass to transform her husband.

When my parents finished having children, I had two older brothers and a younger brother and sister. My earliest memories of home are of my terrified Mom with us little children huddled around her to shield her from Dad. We really believed that we could protect her, and often took along with her whatever abuse Dad had to inflict. One time when Dad threw a full can of beer at Mom, it struck 6-year-old Louie, Jr., on the forehead as he attempted to protect her. The gash required stitches. Sometimes my brother raced to the bathroom during Dad's rages and would vomit. I had a hard time understanding my dad's violence or why he seemed to spend more time screaming than talking.

Later in life I began to realize that it was his own cry of pain to the world. Besides the agony of his childhood, he suffers from scoliosis, a disease of the spinal column that produces a hunched back. The constant physical pain eventually required two surgeries. He also has silicosis, a degeneration of the lungs caused by silica dust lodging in the tissues. Years of working in sweatshop conditions in a ceramics factory in the Los Angeles suburb of Pacoima had caused the disease. There he mixed silica-laden clay without the protection of a breathing mask. Even today he lives with a continual asthmatic cough that at times debilitates him, especially when he catches a cold. The two illnesses left my dad totally disabled by the age of 28, plunging us into the world of government welfare programs.

All through my childhood I struggled with the constant fear that Dad would either die of illness or kill my mom during one of his drunken rages. Each of my siblings grew up scarred because of the continual crisis of life at home. One day I realized something that each of us had in common: we often thought it was our fault that Mom and Dad were having problems. *If we could only behave better,* we would think, *then Mom and Dad would get along with each other.*

One particularly bad day Dad became so abusive that Mom in desperation yanked off her engagement and wedding rings and bent them. Turning to me, she told me to flush them down the toilet. I still remember taking the warped rings into the bathroom and then pretending to dispose of them. Running into my room, I put the rings into my secret little box of treasures under the bed. Then I returned to where my parents now struggled with what they thought was the loss of their wedding symbols. My dad exploded even worse than before.

Like my brothers Louie and Gerry had done on other occasions, I went to my parents and stood in front of them. Tears streaming down my face, I begged them to forgive me for being such a bad boy. Pleading with them to give me just one more chance, I sobbed that I would be "good" again. Then they could stay together and save their marriage. I looked into my mother's incredulous eyes and said, "Mamá, what's wrong with me? Why do I make you and Dad fight so much?" The guilt that children assume by blaming themselves for situations that are out of their control is all too common in abusive families.

My siblings and I were no exception.

One night when I was 6 years old our family visited with friends until very late. We did not start home until 1:00 in the morning. My dad, who was driving and already drunk, suddenly announced that he wanted a drink. In spite of my mom's pleadings he pulled over into a raunchy bar about a half mile from our house. I sat in the front seat with Mom as my siblings slept quietly in the back. The silence rang in our ears after Dad turned off the engine and disappeared into the bar. As I looked at my mom, the single light bulb from the bar entrance reflected in her eyes. She was crying, and I didn't know what to do. After a long time, almost a half hour, I turned to her and said, "I'll be right back."

Before she could stop me, I slipped out of the car and raced across the parking lot. The smoke-filled bar had about 15 customers in various stages of consciousness. Urine reeked at the doorway and garbage was strewn across the floor. Finally, through the hazy dimness I could see my father sitting on a tall stool, far down the length of a very high counter. Drinking from a large cold mug of beer, he seemed to be lost in thought as he stared intently at the wall in front of him. When I crossed the room to where he sat, the whole place went silent. The sight of a small child inside the bar at 1:30 a.m. was more than some of the people could take.

My dad looked at me with shock, not expecting to see one of his children at that moment in that place. I remember feeling determined and strained my little neck to look directly up into his eyes as I said, "Can we go home now? Mommy is really sad, and we all want to go home to sleep." People in the bar expressed either shock or laughter as they heard me. Some said, "Take your wife and kids home!" while others chided, "You're not going to let yourself be bossed around by a little kid, are you?" One guy even went as far as to say, "Slap that kid for coming into a bar this late at night!" Luckily for me, my father didn't understand English.

Dad hesitated, then after a long silence he told me to go back to the car and wait. When I returned to the car my mom realized that things were getting tense outside as drunks, entering and exiting, noticed her—a young woman—in the car. She made a difficult decision and asked us to get out of the car.

After a few moments, when she thought it was safe, we stumbled out into the damp cold and walked home in the early-morning darkness.

Such incidents were sadly all too common. We might find Dad on the front lawn in the morning not knowing where the car was, or we might have to go bail him out of jail. Dad was severely depressed, very ill, and had extremely limited employment opportunities. Angry at the world for his lot in life, he moved us around from house to house throughout the Los Angeles area. We lived in three different houses in Lincoln Heights, and at least one frightening apartment for a short time in Pacoima. There a neighbor woman would occasionally force her terrified little 4-year-old boy to sleep outside in the car all night to punish him. Once we lived in a house in the suburb of Sunland, where we found some stability because friends helped my parents buy the house.

I knew that both my parents loved me dearly. At times my dad even enjoyed playful moments with us children. But as long as the issues in his life remained unresolved, we paid the price for his problems. I even developed ways of defending Dad as a loyal enabler. What else can little children do when they love their father deeply and yet with the same intensity resent what he does ?

Pancho Villa and the revolutionary war

My father's parents followed Pancho Villa during the Mexican Revolution at the beginning of the twentieth century. Both his mother and father bore the scars of a bloody civil war. My grandmother, as a young woman, often had to hide when Villa's men would enter her village. Although she fully supported the revolution, she had to live with the reality that chaos and evil are the constant conditions endured by those caught in the middle of any war.

Witnessing death and brutality hardened my grandmother toward everyone around her, especially those she loved. My grandfather learned simply to avoid problems by allowing her to develop the tough parameters of my father's childhood home.

My father acquired most of his values in the streets of Ciudad Juarez, Chihuahua. At the age of 13 he began running away from home, being gone for weeks at a time. Life seemed easier in the world than at home. As a teen he became a "Pachuco," or gang member, in Juarez. Having many close calls with the law, he often found himself in the center of trouble in his neighborhood. When he fell in love with my mother, he wanted to settle down to a new life. Three months pregnant, my mom married him at the courthouse in Tijuana in 1958.

My father brought my mom and started his family in the United States for the same reason that all immigrants come to this land. Whether it was 200 years ago or two days ago, people flock to the U.S. to make a life in a land of opportunity. My mom particularly felt at home because her father, who had also espoused the Mexican Revolution with Pancho Villa, had spent a significant portion of his life in Texas. My maternal grandmother lived in Chicago the first part of her life, then married my grandfather in Fort Worth, Texas, in 1928. Fleeing the economic depression in the United States the next year, they returned to Mexico.

Although my mom was born and raised in Mexico, she grew up hearing her parents speak perfect English. During her childhood she lived on the Juarez, Mexico, side of the border, yet she crossed into El Paso, Texas, almost daily. My mom's father had dual citizenship and worked at Fort Bliss, the American Army base just across the river. Her mother and most of her siblings had jobs at various times in the United States and were citizens also. American Army soldiers were frequent guests at my mom's home during her childhood.

One morning when my mother was 12 years old, she watched her mother die tragically of a heart attack. My grandmother was only 36, and my mom tells us that, as a child, being left without a mother was the single most difficult crisis of her life. A few months later, on New Year's eve, as she, her father, and her siblings were driving home from El Paso, they were involved in a horrific car accident. A drunk driver on the wrong side of the road crashed into their Model T Ford head-on at high speed. Everyone had severe injuries, and her father died. My mom was an orphan at the age of 13. She had to leave school and assume the role of homemaker for all her older siblings, who now had to work every day.

Because of their untimely deaths, my grandparents never completed the paperwork on my mom's citizenship. All but one of her siblings had U.S. citizenship and jobs. When my parents moved to Los Angeles, they had to go through the naturalization process, becoming American citizens in 1966. All of us, their children, were born in the U.S. as citizens. Gerry and Louie were born in El Paso, while Ruben, Martha, and I were born in Los Angeles.

My parents had come to Los Angeles searching for opportunity, but my dad soon discovered that it was very limited. Jobs were scarce and most were low-paying, providing no medical or job safety. Some of our friends found jobs as domestic servants for middle- and upper-class families while others were fortunate enough to find good blue-collar jobs at large factories. The latter were the hardest for people of color to obtain.

All of this naturally affected us as a family in Los Angeles. To add to all the tensions of life at home, I also struggled to know who I was. Children who constantly blame themselves for the trauma around them soon lack personal identity and develop low self-esteem. That was the first layer of my childhood. The next layer was about to come . . . school.

My siblings and I entered a predominantly Caucasian elementary school, one at a time, as we grew old enough to attend. Gerry and Louie were well into their school experiences when I first started kindergarten in 1965. I spoke no English and had a hard time even knowing what was happening in the classroom. The teacher was a wonderful and patient woman named Mrs. Miller. I could only pronounce her name as "mee-sees moh-lee," which caused lots of laughter when the other children heard my attempts at English. Also I was a chronic bedwetter and couldn't understand why the other children didn't want to stand near me. Soon I heard names like "skunk" and other less desirable labels.

I particularly remember lunchtime. Many children had colorful metal lunch pails filled with neatly wrapped sandwiches, fruit, and juices. When I would pull out my oversized shopping bag and proceed to unwrap a bean burrito from an aluminum foil sheet, children would often erupt into laughter. This was long before Taco Bell restaurants and the popularity of the burrito. Most of the kids had never seen one before and joked that I was eating "skunk food."

After a particularly embarrassing episode in which a larger

number of children than usual made fun of me, I went to the trash can and threw my burrito away. The crowd of kids cheered wildly in their victory, and from then on I quietly threw my burrito away every day, just before lunchtime. After a few weeks, somehow, as always, my mom found out about it and developed a solution. She bought loaves of Wonder bread and made bean sandwiches for me to take to school. It helped a lot.

Being the target of constant jeering by the other children began to have its effect. A crisis developed when the school placed me on a different schedule than my brother Louie. He attended school in the morning, and I went in the afternoon, leaving me absolutely vulnerable to the predator children who would await me at school. I decided to hide in an alley rather than go to school. As I think back today, it was actually quite remarkable that I could sit in an alley for as long as four hours. That's a long time for a small kid!

The school called my mother to ask if I was sick because they had not seen me for several days. Sensing the situation, she promised the principal that I would be back at school soon. The next day after I left home, she followed me quietly at a distance. Once I had settled into my little hiding place in the alley, she suddenly appeared. We looked at each other in silence. Instead of scolding me, my mother knelt and simply held me in her arms. We both began to cry.

After a few moments she asked why I was there. I told her that I didn't want to go to school because the other kids didn't like me. They made fun of me, and I was lost without Louie. The school nurse came by our house later to confirm that I was going to return. Seizing the opportunity, she also advised me of the value of taking daily showers before going to school. My mom then took me to see the principal of the school. There she negotiated with her to have me put back on the morning schedule so that Louie and I could attend together again. From then on I also showered before school each day. My "skunk" days were over.

As I grew older the insults from children became sharper. Whereas very young children joked about skunks and funny-looking food, some of the older ones had developed negative attitudes toward my racial heritage and language. Speaking English took extra effort for me, and I had an accent. The children

16

would often question me about something so they could laugh at my accent. No matter what I said, it was always funny to them. It all seemed harmless to the other parents, who sometimes witnessed their child making fun of me after school. With a giggle, a mother would tell her son or daughter not to do that to me. Obviously she thought that it caused no real harm and seemed rude only in terms of the etiquette she was teaching her child.

The tension increased over time. One boy named Johnny Larson didn't like me. A tough kid, one day he decided that it was time to "beat José up and teach him a lesson." Johnny had two older brothers and a cousin who wanted to be there when he carried out his threat. Each day he tried to fight me. My insecurity at school turned into abject fear.

Several times I barely escaped Johnny's older brothers. One instance occurred on the playground after school. Johnny and his brothers had corralled me into the playground so that I could not escape over the tall fences. I ran into the sports equipment room in the middle of the playground. While I hid there, the playground attendant, Miss Bear, ordered me out of the room. But after one glance at my terrified face, she listened as I told her of Johnny and his brothers waiting outside. She allowed me to stay there for a while until the other boys left.

Johnny became obsessed with beating me up, even betting with other children on what he was going to do to me when the right moment came. One day I made the fateful mistake of walking home through the alley. Johnny had figured out my route home and was waiting there. As I reached the middle portion of the alley, his brothers suddenly appeared at both ends, trapping me. As I saw Johnny's cousin appear with a strange smile on his face, I honestly wondered if I was going to die. My heart wanted to stop, and my terror became indescribable as I began to shake and the palms of my hands became damp and cold. I tried to speak, but I was so frightened that I could manage only a series of strange sounds.

Abruptly Johnny pushed me from behind, and I fell to the pavement. He then shouted that I was a "dirty Mexican" and painfully kicked me in a way that I would rather not describe. I struggled to understand what was happening to me, unable to comprehend what was so dirty about my race. Children are highly impressionable and easily affected by every experience in life. Racism causes wounds that take a long time to heal. I staggered to my feet and again tried to escape, but Johnny's older brothers and cousin caught me.

Trapped and desperate, I turned around and jumped on Johnny Larson with the adrenaline that comes only in extreme emergencies. I still remember the painful surprise on his face as I desperately attacked him out of my fear and frustration. I then proceeded to rearrange his facial features.

Johnny's brothers grabbed me, restraining my arms from behind. Now Johnny could do some of his own resculpting of my face. I screamed in terror and begged for mercy. He hit and kicked me repeatedly with a look of sheer delight on his face. I shouted that I was sorry for hitting him and promised, "I will never touch you again." Fortunately, a man who had heard the commotion, ran out of his house to break up the fight. Everyone scattered and ran out of the alley. Both Johnny and I were crying, he from joy and I from humiliation. The emotional pain hurt much more than the physical.

For the first time in my life someone had violently made their point that my race was inferior. The prejudice I had experienced earlier at school regarding my food or accent was something I felt I could teach other children to understand. But the blunt racism of someone who felt superior to me just because of what I looked like on the outside struck at the depths of my very being. I walked home with a deep sense of loneliness.

Entering the house, I washed my face and told my mom that I had fallen down. Of course, with shoeprints on my shirt, she knew better. Yet she did not make an issue of it, deciding to wait until I felt better and could talk about it. Going outside, I sat in the thick grass of our front lawn to nurse my wounds.

Suddenly Johnny's cousin showed up, looking very upset. "Johnny is not going to rest until he kills you," he said. A pain knifed deep in my chest, I asked, "Why?" The boy told me that I had crossed the line and that I should not have hit Johnny, because it "wasn't right for a Mexican to do that." He also informed me that the word was out about what I had done and that others were going to make me pay as well. Realizing that the situation was getting further out of hand, I decided to try to end the crisis by adopting a posture of defeat. Fighting back tears, I told him that I knew my place and that I had lacked respect for Johnny. I said that I was very much afraid of him and that I would always tell anyone who asked me that "Johnny beat me up fair and square."

"You'll tell people that Johnny won?" the cousin demanded.

"Yes," I replied mournfully. Too ashamed, I could not tell my mom what I had said to Johnny's cousin.

At school several kids confronted me about the fight, and I dutifully told them that I was afraid of Johnny because he had already beat me up once. Finally one kid shoved me and said, "Why don't you go back where you came from!" I was again confused, knowing that I had been born in the United States like almost all the children in the school. The kid shouted further that I should go back to Mexico, where all "wet-backs" belong. "You're not an American," another boy added, "and my dad says you people only cause trouble." "Everything was fine until Mexicans came to our school!" a girl shouted.

My isolation and uncertainty continued for quite a while. About a month after the fight I walked by Johnny's house as he opened the gate to his yard. He had two large German shepherd dogs. The one he released was named Tina. As I froze in fear, Tina calmly trotted over to where I was standing and, with a growl, clamped her teeth into my right thigh. Johnny and his brothers stood laughing, so their mother ran to where I was screaming as the dog continued to bite me.

She pulled the animal off me and apologized as we both examined the blood on my pants. I discovered that day that dog bites really hurt. They cause painful bruising that stays with you for quite a while. *Didn't she see that her son had released the dog on purpose?* I wondered. The dog bite and the memory of the fight and its aftermath reminded me of the danger of racial violence if I got careless on the street. Johnny didn't seem to realize that it was no longer necessary to pursue me and keep me constantly humiliated. I now assumed a submissive role simply to avoid conflict. But those experiences tore at me inside.

After the dog incident my mom had had enough and went over to Johnny's house to talk with his mother. I thought my mom would be angry, but she looked more alarmed than anything else. She paused outside their chain-link fence while Johnny's mom stood just inside, flanked by the large dogs that barked loudly only inches from her. I remember feeling

19

extremely moved by my mother's courage, because I thought the Larsons were not the kind of people who would respond to peaceful overtures. From a distance I watched the two women talking and still to this day don't know what they said.

My mother appeared very calm as they spoke to each other. I have never in my life seen my mother angry toward another person either in retaliation or response to injustice. She consistently taught us that to fight physically only increased the disgrace and worsened the problem. After they finished talking, I never again had to hide from Johnny, his brothers, or his German shepherd dogs. Also I never again in my life lifted my hand to strike another person, even when I found myself in trouble because of injustice. To hit someone, even when we feel they deserve it, only invites more trouble. I thank God that I learned early from a long-suffering mother the value of turning the other cheek. Incredibly, over time, Johnny became my friend.

My problems at school did not result from a lack of friends. Each of my siblings found quality friendships among the students. I too had a few good friends, but always some made it their duty to inform me that I was not one of them. I could not deal with the bizarre nature of racism and the rejection that comes with it. The experiences left their mark on me. As I experienced pain and confusion both at home and school, I increasingly lost my personal identity and my self-esteem plummeted. The same survival mechanisms that served me at home I now began to fall back upon at school. Again I asked my mom tearfully, "Mamá, what's wrong with me? Why do I speak Spanish? Why do I eat different food?" Again I blamed myself for something I could not control. I apologized to others for *their* bigotry and sought forgiveness for *their* misbehavior.

Martin Luther King—"I have a dream . . ."

But by the time I was 8 or 9 years old glimmers of hope began to appear. They came in different ways. One day as I watched the *Flintstones* cartoon show on television a special news announcement interrupted the program. A somber voice said that "the Reverend Dr. Martin Luther King, Jr., had been shot." I called my mom and siblings and asked, "Who is Martin Luther King?" My mother said he was an important man that had helped many people. After a short time the announcer declared that King had died from his gunshot wound.

For the rest of the evening most of the channels showed newsreel clips of King's life, introducing me to concepts that have stayed with me throughout the rest of my life. I watched as police used German shepherd dogs to attack helpless people trying to cross a bridge on a walk to Montgomery. Other scenes depicted violence against men and women who wanted to register to vote. One image that particularly inspired me was that of a line of dignified men marching quietly in Memphis, each wearing a sign that read "I am a man." Still other footage showed King in jail and police clubbings in Chicago. Quickly I identified with the plight of African-Americans, because I immediately knew that my experiences were similar.

Then the TV presented a large portion of the "I Have a Dream" speech King delivered on the steps of the Lincoln Memorial in Washington, D.C. He was by far the most powerful speaker I had ever heard. While I was too young to understand much of what he said, I never forgot the words "when all of God's children, Black men and White men, Jews and Gentiles, Catholics and Protestants, will all join in the words of that old Negro spiritual, 'free at last, free at last, thank God almighty, I'm free at last!'" Although he didn't mention Brown men, I knew Martin Luther King included me, because he spoke of *all* God's children! Those scenes on our television after King's tragic death provided the ray of hope that would shape my future and help me to relate to the world in a nonviolent way.

My immediate problem was that I was increasingly retreating from life into my own little world. I was disappearing ever further into solitude and isolation. While I am naturally an extrovert, my family and friends noticed me becoming more distant and introverted. For example, at the age of 8 I received my first microscope and chemistry set. My mother found them in a yard sale and thought that at least one of her children would enjoy them. I turned out to be the one who quickly picked them up to explore the world of science.

Smoke and stink bombs drove the family out of the house more than once during the next few months. The complexity of chemical reactions and my ability to control them especially intrigued me. Many unfortunate bugs also found themselves experiencing the "Rojas torture lab" for analysis under my microscope. I had my own "house of horrors" made up of a large collection of insect wings, eyes, legs, and other body parts.

My uncle Francisco gave me a professional watch repair kit and, after ruining two of my uncle's perfectly good Swiss watches, I learned to make simple repairs. The tiny moving parts fascinated me. I would switch watch faces and other parts, creating my own watches! Although not all of my attempts worked, I learned that I could do well in a setting in which I could creatively make things happen.

My mom—always the keen observer of her children—watched me closely. She developed a new nickname for me during this phase of my life. One day while I was intently working on one of my many little projects she asked, "How's 'my dreamer'?" I looked at her and asked what she meant.

"You're always dreaming of new things, *mijo* [son]" she said, "and you always do them in your own special way." I felt good inside. A creative environment enabled me to find true happiness. And it also kept me safely away from other kids at school, avoiding that source of pain in my life. As for the pain at home, it too became partially manageable when I retreated into solitude to work on my "science stuff."

My brother Louie survived by disappearing with his friends. By being out of the house, pursuing friends and sports, he felt that he could cope just a little better. At times he seemed more like a defiant preadolescent, but appearances can be deceiving. His trauma was real, and if he didn't do something about it, he knew he could not cope. Gerry did not fare as well. After my dad attacked violently one time too many, Gerry moved out of our house and lived with my aunt across town. It devastated my mother. She missed him horribly, but was afraid of what could happen if Dad carried out any of the many things he threatened to do to my brother. My father had hurt him physically and emotionally for so long that Mom couldn't take any more chances.

Although Gerry came to visit often, even spending weekends with us, he never again lived with us full time. I spent time with him whenever I could, whether at my aunt's house or at our home. Yet my life was never again to be the same. A part of it had vanished, and I could do nothing about it. I now felt myself drawn to Gerry with the profound bond of a child who refuses to let his eldest brother go.

As Gerry grew older, he became strong and muscular. He had a wonderful, playful personality and developed a special leadership streak. From an early age he had demonstrated a clear ability to lead others. People felt themselves naturally drawn to him. Of course, if anyone resisted, Gerry could easily clarify his role with a strong hand—a *very* strong hand. Now that our dad had disowned him, Gerry quickly sharpened his leadership skills, even though it may have been for the wrong reasons. There are leaders who lead great, others are great leaders. Gerry was the latter. He became my hero, a guy who hid his pain with a tough exterior. One day I decided that I wanted to be "just like Gerry."

In 1969 my father had two back surgeries. The curvature in his spine was pinching some nerves. Several times a week he would suffer sudden severe leg cramps. Whether at night while in bed or in the middle of the supermarket, his legs would go into knots, and he would scream in pain. We would do our best to help by massaging his legs, but he simply had to endure the pain until the cramps would subside. The surgeries relieved the pressure on the spinal nerves, thus ending the leg cramps.

On my ninth birthday Dad was recovering from his second surgery, and my birthday wish was to go see him at the hospital. Mom agreed, but said that on the way she wanted to drop something off at a friend's house. When we entered the friend's home, I was greeted with a surprise party! About a dozen children attended, and it was the first party of major significance held for me. It didn't matter that the cake was about six inches in diameter, providing each of us only a symbolic sliver of cake. I remember laughing loudly and literally being "out of myself" with delight. My mom could see that I was capable of coming out my shell under special circumstances.

After the party we went to see Dad at the Orthopedic Hospital across town. Excitedly I ran into the room and, before he could tell me to stop, slammed my head into his stomach in an attempt to hug him. I did not know what a full body cast was, but I painfully learned that day that it is something as hard as rock around a person's body. My dad had a body cast from his waist to his neck. The huge bump on my head testified to that. But that birthday clearly ranked as one of the happiest days of my childhood. I had a party held in my honor and my dad was sober, subdued, and loving, happy to be surrounded by his family at the hospital. It was all so magical.

Our family had now established itself into a typical pattern of long-term dysfunction. Dad's ill health, the joblessness, government welfare, racial prejudice, helplessness, and hopelessness would fuel his anger and our fear, eventually leading to an explosion. Then we would recover somewhat, only to repeat the process again.

However, God in His great love and mercy had a plan. The Lord heard our cry and reached out to us. I was to discover that one of the greatest ways God comes to most of us is through other people. We often underestimate the power of the mentor relationship, but people are His greatest resource in this world.

During that next year the most significant transition of our lives occurred. Like nothing before then, it would dramatically reshape my family's future. The Seventh-day Adventist Church reached out and touched us—literally.

THAT WHICH IS RIGHT BEFORE GOD

Our family roots go back for centuries in what is now the southwestern United States. Almost 200 years before the first English-speaking Pilgrims landed on Plymouth Rock, my ancestors already spoke Spanish. The Spanish conquerors who had settled our native lands not only intermarried with our race and gave us the Spanish language, they also brought Catholic missionaries.

Consequently, Catholicism defined my family's view of the world for almost 400 years. However, most of my extended family express their faith in a way that goes beyond religious beliefs. Catholicism is a cultural reality that pervades Latino cultures. It touches every aspect of our lives, even among those who might not be formally religious. In many ways to be Latino is to be Catholic. Consequently, when the first Seventh-day Adventists touched us, my parents were obviously worried and extremely cautious about them.

Francisco and Jesucita Madrid—Adventists with an attitude

We had known Francisco and Jesucita Madrid for years. They had helped us by selling us their little house. My parents referred to them with traditional Mexican respect by addressing them with titles that included their nicknames. Francisco was "Don Pancho," and Jesusita was "Dona Chuy." The "Don" designation, much as in Italian tradition, is a title of great respect for our elders.

The couple had more than once made a holiday meaningful by the timely delivery of food or other gifts. If they could not come themselves, they would send others with the food. One of those families brought us food on Christmas, a day I will never forget. Adventist Community Services was more than a mere "quilting operation." The Madrids made sure that it was the hands and feet of Jesus to our family.

On several occasions Don Pancho had been awakened in the late hours of the night to find us somewhere in Los Angeles. The setting was always similar. The car had broken down, with our family in it, during another of Dad's late-night barhopping runs. Don Pancho would pile my mom and us five children into the cab of his pickup truck, leaving Dad to ride outside in the cold. My father usually sobered up as the chilly wind blew through his hair on the way home.

The Madrids became like parents to my parents and were among the few on the planet who could actually scold my dad and get his attention. They entertained us in their home frequently as guests and made it clear they loved us. The Madrids were Seventh-day Adventists with an attitude. Their faith was not a continual proclamation of doctrines, but about living Jesus and demonstrating His love in a way that made Him come to life!

Many do not realize that people's perceptions of Jesus are directly shaped by their experiences with those who claim to love Him. When people who say they know Jesus live in ways that do not reflect Him, it makes Jesus a liar to those with whom they come in contact. Consequently, as people reflect the love of Jesus in their lives, He becomes a tangible Saviour for others. The Madrids revealed the character of Jesus each time they reached out to us.

Don Pancho and Dona Chuy succeeded in winning our hearts. Our relationship with them grew over time. When the Madrids later sent someone to invite us children to Vacation Bible School, my mom at first hesitated. But the fact that their church had done so much to meet our family's needs convinced her that she could trust it in the lives of the Rojas children. We went to Vacation Bible School and enjoyed every minute. I did not own a Bible, but I found that I could memorize scriptures easily and liked winning the little items the teachers offered as rewards. Since I usually won a comb for my efforts, I wondered if there was any symbolism attached to that particular prize.

Pastor Byron Spears—For righteousness' sake . . .

In 1970 an Adventist evangelist, Pastor Byron Spears, held a series of meetings in Van Nuys, across the San Fernando Valley. The Madrids invited us, and we all attended. A local pastor, Ron Howell, led the songs with triumphant enthusiasm! They also gave out gifts as door prizes for sitting in a particular seat, and then Pastor Spears preached with incredible power.

Having suffered from polio earlier in life, Pastor Spears walked with the aid of two canes. He would slowly approach the podium and then place 10 neatly folded handkerchiefs on the top. By the end of his sermon he had used all 10 of those handkerchiefs to wipe the sweat from his face. He preached totally from memory, including huge portions of Scripture that he would sometimes intentionally misstate just to see if we were following in our Bibles. The conviction the man spoke with is something I still attempt to emulate today, for I too now preach totally from memory. Like Dr. Martin Luther King, Jr., before him, another Black preacher was making an important impact on my life.

One night they called my mom's name from the front as the winner of the Bible for that meeting. What made that moment significant is that Dad had years earlier thrown her Catholic Bible out of the house into the ivy in our yard. We knew that the Bible would not be very welcome at home. The audience turned to see who Stella Rojas was. My embarrassed mom then turned to me and whispered, "Why don't you go up and get the Bible, mijo?"

Quickly I ran down the aisle to the front. Pastor Howell handed me a beautiful Bible, bound in a soft white cover and wrapped in plastic. He had one of those ear-to-ear smiles that would melt anyone. Shaking my hand, he told me to "tell your mama congratulations for us," prompting an approving giggle from the audience. I held that Bible to my heart and triumphantly walked down the aisle, with big strides, back to my seat. Mom let each of her children look at the wrapped King James Bible and then handed it back to me to take care of.

I remember clutching it to my chest for the rest of that evening. As we drove home that night, I still held that Bible to my heart. Then, somewhere in the darkness between Roscoe Boulevard and the Golden State Freeway, I raised that wrapped Bible to my face and reverently kissed the cover. The Word of God had entered my life. I reveled in the thought of knowing that God cared for me. That same Bible is still at my parent's house today. The scribbles of little children fill the old and very worn volume. It is probably one of the greatest treasures in the family.

Not long after that, Pastor Spears asked people to give their lives to Christ and prepare for the joy of baptism. He often challenged us to take steps to follow Jesus "for righteousness' sake." The call to baptism was simple: "Take a step for righteousness, and be baptized." That night I turned to my oldest brother Gerry and asked, "What do you think? Should we be baptized?"

Without hesitation he said, "Yeah, man! Pastor Spears and Pastor Howell are *vatos locos*. I think we should be baptized." *Vatos locos* literally translates as "crazy dudes," which on the streets of Los Angeles is an extremely flattering compliment. My brother meant that he thought the two pastors were some of the greatest people in the world. God had led them to reach us with the gospel of Christ. Louie and mom also made their decisions for baptism that same night. The Madrids wept for joy!

When the day of the baptismal service arrived, Gerry did not show up. He had changed his mind. On March 28, 1970, two days after my birthday, Louie, Mom, and I entered the water and were baptized together. Dad sat in the audience with my younger siblings Ruben and Martha. Our denominational commitment seemed a subtle transition, but that day signaled new directions and new hopes for us. No electrical charge or mysterious chill ran down my spine. I just knew that the time had come to make my decision and that I had done the right thing.

I was 10 years old, too young by some people's standards for baptism. Yet I must say that the issue of age in baptism has never been a problem to me. By the age of 10 I had already spent time with Gerry on the streets of Los Angeles. A member of the Big Hazard gang, he had introduced me to his friends and on more than one occasion I had been present when they used alcohol or other drugs. Since Gerry was my hero, I absorbed his values and wanted to eventually share his experiences. While I had not yet tried drugs or alcohol, circumstances were leading dangerously to an eventual curiosity about them.

Being baptized at the age of 10 involved more than a discussion about whether I was too young or not. It became a critical tool in God's hand, giving me a conscience, a commitment in my life to that which is right before Him. Many times during the years to come the thought of my baptism kept me from doing many tempting things on the street with Gerry. Indeed, I can honestly say that baptism was the first of several experiences that God used to save my life.

We were now Seventh-day Adventists, and my dad was not happy about it. He decreed that we could not go to church on Saturday. At the same time he suddenly resented the Adventists who would come to visit. Except for Don Pancho and Dona Chuy, Adventists were welcome in our home. My mother was not about to stay away from church, however. She had people wait for us down the street on Saturday mornings and we would quietly slip out the back door to attend church.

Of course, things would often get ugly when we returned home to an angry father. The tense weekly confrontations about church continued for a while. Finally, one day my dad asked, "What is it that you guys do at the church that you have to go every week?" His question seemed to arise out of desperation because of his inability to get us to stop attending. Quickly I answered, "Why don't you come with us and see for yourself?" My dad went to church with us the next weekend that summer of 1970, and has been attending ever since!

Dad was baptized the next December on a crisp, sunny California winter day. The closest church with a baptistry was the La Crescent church, and it was there that Dad took his step of commitment. Fresh snow covered the mountains, and amidst that backdrop we celebrated Dad's new start. Like us, he had accepted a new beginning. The scenery reflected the day. Just as that winter day, surrounded by snowy mountains, still had temperatures reaching into the 70s in the city, God took the cold winter of my dad's life and brought the warmth of His presence. God had reached into Dad's soul and given him a real reason for living. I was deliriously happy!

During the next few years new horizons brought new opportunities for the Rojas family. The biggest blessing that resulted from my dad's commitment to God was the end of his alcoholic binges. We had no more drunken, terror-filled nights and days, no more painful whippings with his belt. No longer did we find the police in our front yard. Such changes were the firstfruits of Dad's new life. I still thank God for the miracle of His grace in my father's experience. No one else could have changed him as God did. The Lord took Dad's heart of stone and gave him a heart of flesh.

Of course, I do not mean to suggest that we were suddenly happy, holy, and free of trouble at home. But it did put us onto a new path that gave us better options for life. We began to have family worship every day. Singing songs of praise in the living room, we read from Scripture and memorized large portions for the sheer joy of grasping God's Word.

The devil predictably increased his efforts to disrupt us. Because a family with our level of dysfunction often has deep-seated tendencies to addictive behavior, Satan worked to give us "new addictions" within our newfound faith. We had a great beginning, but not a year had passed before an extremist off-shoot group brought us new and addictive restrictions that they called "true Christian living."

They systematically taught during their frequent visits that God demanded a stringent lifestyle from us if we were to be saved. Being spiritual infants, we could not discern all the complications it would bring to our home. One of the joys of real Seventh-day Adventism is the role of healthy living as an experience of God's grace in our bodies. Another is Sabbath observance within the context of loving and serving others. These individuals, however, brought unending demands to behave in certain ways or face certain doom.

At first we assumed that they were members of our church, but soon they increased their condemnation of the denomination. As we spent more time with them, we realized that they were not Adventists after all. They referred to our church as "the big church," often comparing it to Babylon and other evil symbols from prophecy. I now realize that many of them had gone through painful and addictive experiences in their own lives and brought that same kind of behavior to their faith. For example, some of them feel a continual and absolute bitterness toward life, people, and the church. No one ever seems to meet their requirements for Christian behavior and they often condemn almost everyone, because most have obviously strayed from "the truth."

Some people replace a commitment to Christ that produces love and a humble life of service with an addiction to religious behavior that creates frustration and impatience with almost everyone. Some even display anger and hate in the name of Jesus. As I look at this today, I realize that many of the members of these groups, having known nothing but condemnation from those around them, naturally conclude that they in turn should be judgmental toward others.

We could not see it at first, but our encounter led to a short but frustrating spiritual detour for our family. It seems outrageous and extremely unfair that a family that had endured as much pain as we had should be the target of one of these independent groups so early after our baptism. Such factions rarely do any direct evangelism in the community. Instead, they approach those new in the church and cause division and confusion.

Sure enough, instead of us growing in Christ, the new addictions diverted us into new struggles. For example, my father turned from alcoholism to the idea that milk products are sinful. Somehow, instead of helping us to experience the joy of Christ each day, our visitors taught us such ideas as rejecting meat and dairy products and viewing negatively anyone who ate them. One of their people even insisted that using soap was a sin because it irritated the human skin! Obviously he stood alone in life since his odor was not the most pleasant. We began to live as if with a scorecard to see if we were fulfilling everything that God demanded of us, hoping that maybe we might be worthy of salvation someday.

The devastation that the new rules caused on some of us children as we now entered puberty was terrible. The sudden loss of family gatherings at the ice cream parlor or the occasional submarine sandwich had their impact. Rebellion quickly developed among us. Ruben and Martha were still quite small, but Louie, Gerry, and I could not be easily caged. Many times we sneaked a doughnut or ice cream on the streets. The guilt we experienced over such simple things still shocks me. I am fully convinced that God never intended for His children to feel so trapped and imprisoned by such an oppressive lifestyle.

The issue is clearly one of attitude. I am a vegetarian on a low-fat, low-cholesterol diet, excited about contributing to my health through a wonderful health message such as ours. My greatest joy is that this lifestyle is an actual result of a life with Christ and not merely an attempt to win His favor. What makes Adventism so wonderful to me is that God's love is an experience of a joyful way of life. To condemn the mote in someone else's eye can cause a desperate blindness in which a person will not notice the bigger and more grievous sin—the beam in their own eye. I cannot fathom judging another, because that would hurt my own experience with Jesus.

We had been baptized because we wanted to experience the gospel of Christ. But having fallen under the influence of the off-shoot, we now had to find a way to survive yet another nightmare. Louie again suffered. One day he was punished for eating white bread instead of the appropriate seven-grain bread. The occasional milk shakes he sneaked after school became a source of extreme guilt for him too. Such cruelty fostered in the name of God suggested that He is a terrible task master and that we are not His children but His unwilling slaves. Living healthy lifestyles will always come best from a healthy relationship with God.

Gerry avoided all this by simply staying away from the family more and more. Since he lived with my aunt he had no trouble looking elsewhere for stability. Eventually he joined the larger, more fearsome Clover gang in East Los Angeles. In existence since the 1950s, it now has more than 2,000 members. Slipping into serious drug abuse, Gerry began a long list of arrests for a wide array of crimes. During his sophomore year he dropped out of high school and never again returned. Although a star gymnast at Lincoln High School, he simply left everything behind for his gang. I remember hearing that he had gotten a girl pregnant somewhere in town and that she had had a little girl she named Priscilla. To this day I have never seen or met her. My unknown niece is now in her late 20s and there is no way that we can find her today in the vast concrete jungles of Los Angeles.

My parents grew more confused because they wanted our happiness. Yet the independent people pressured them to be "firm" with us. Slowly it wore down my resistance to the new rules. Perhaps because of my inexperience in life I absorbed them more easily. Soon I began to find fault with others also and stopped listening to a sermon for what it offered in the way of growth and blessing. Instead, at the age of 12 I began to scrutinize each sermon I'd hear to see if it contained accurate truth. I learned less about God and now tried to make sure everybody else was hearing what the offshoot group told me were God's rules. Soon I stopped experiencing true worship and praise. Life was becoming an exercise of finding fault in others, leading to increasing frustration, and all in the name of Jesus.

Once more Louie withdrew to the comfort of his friends and sports activities. It was a relief for him to be away from the house. I went back to my microscope, chemistry set, and watches. Also I began to add musical instruments to my solitary world as well as a growing interest in drawing and painting. Mom knew that things were not well. She worried constantly but did not know what to do about it. Our visitors said that the "truth" required us to live in such sadness as a sign of our commitment to God.

Pastor Kingsley Miniffie—Patiently praying for us . . .

With each passing day the pressures of our oppressive lifestyle continued to take their toll on each of us in his or her own way. The Adventist Church sought to help but by then we had learned to avoid them. Pastor Kingsley Miniffie, our church pastor, would visit and encourage us to participate in church activities. But the offshoots warned us to ignore him. He was a saintly man, patiently praying for us as a family and consistently ministering to us whether we welcomed him or not. Quietly he shed tears outside in his car as he asked God to find a way to touch our family even if he could not. The Miniffies compassionately ministered to us and never ceased their efforts to help us.

Just as before, God had a plan in mind to further heal my family. The Lord was not about to let us go that easily. We were to experience another transition that would eventually resolve many of the issues troubling our family. God continued to preserve our family through several more painful experiences.

The first challenge came when my dad won a suit against

the ceramics factory over the debilitating lung disease he had acquired when working there without protection. With great hope my parents invested the money at a savings and loan institution in town. Within only a few weeks, however, it declared bankruptcy, and our family lost most of the money. After lengthy procedures my parents managed to recover a small portion of it, but it was a crushing blow to my dad, who had hoped to make something out of the pain of his disability by investing the first real money our family ever had.

Then my parents heard from a family in the mountains of northern California who invited us to join them as they practiced "true education" and "present truth" in the world of nature. Our visitors said that the money we had left would be sufficient for us to live in the less expensive mountains. Soon we moved from Los Angeles to a gorgeous northern California place called Hoaglin Valley in the Trinity Alps south of Mount Shasta. It was quite different from what we had known in the city of Los Angeles. The site was accessible only by dirt road and a two-hour drive from the nearest small village. Pine trees provided the dominant scent and sounds as the wind blew across the forest. Wild animals often visited the property where our trailer stood at the foot of a meadow. One did not hear an ambulance or a police siren for 40 miles in any direction.

Living there was like going to heaven, and things went well for the first couple weeks. The family that had invited us there seemed nice and life appeared peaceful. We paid rent for living on the mountain and looked forward to many years of happiness. The occasional mule deer, bear, or mountain lion wandering across the meadow by our little trailer only added to the incredible experience. That wilderness had a special intimacy that I will never forget. In the short time we lived there I acquired a love for wild medicinal herbs and other natural remedies.

Then abruptly my parents had to pay for many unforeseen costs. We received invoices for everything from school tuition for classes that never happened, to costs for "materials" that we could not identify. I recall being present when my parents shook hands on a deal for a new electric generator. Since the mountain had no electric service, the residents had to have a generator for their homes. My father paid for a new generator, but when it arrived, our hosts gave us their old used one instead. My parents quickly protested the injustice of the situation. Then I remember the head of our host family sternly explaining that this was an example of our "responsibility to support the present truth for these days." I watched them bring the faulty used generator to our house, then install the new state-of-the-art generator that we had paid for at their home.

Tensions grew as our family did not readily accept the new list of restrictive beliefs they unveiled during the three months that we lived there. It appeared that the head of our host family wanted to start his own church and envisioned a compound of sorts on the mountain. He spoke often of a plan to bring many families to the "school." One day he announced that he was the fulfillment of "the voice crying in the wilderness to prepare the way of the Lord" spoken of in the book of Joel. Again we realized too late that our hosts were not Seventh-day Adventists. Daily, things became more frightening.

At the same time as the electric generator transaction, we had placed a down payment of $1,000 with our hosts for a five-acre lot. It was a beautiful property that we intended to move our trailer to during the next few months. That $1,000 was also the last money we possessed. By 1972 standards it was a lot of money. Somehow we had been led to believe that we could still earn enough money on the mountain to support ourselves. When we had the land measured, it turned out to be less than an acre in size. When we again confronted our host family with our concerns, they denied that there was any problem. Then my father asked for a refund of the precious $1,000. At that point everything collapsed.

The host family appeared sincere, but obviously did not have well-laid plans for successfully conducting a community. They certainly did not know how to run a school either. After a tension-filled month, bitter winter storms began. It was the coldest winter in decades, with unusually heavy snows and cold temperatures.

Our host family began to behave in a peculiar way. Then a few weeks later, to our shock, they abandoned us on the mountain. The host family simply packed up and moved away, leaving us literally in the cold! We had never experienced snow before, and now found ourselves living in an old 8' by 30' trailer covered by three feet of snow. Temperatures dipped as low as

-5° F for several nights. Having spent all of our money, we faced a real emergency. Word spread among the few mountain folk that the "city family" had been left alone to fend for themselves on the ridge. That made as much sense as one of the mountain families finding themselves stranded without their four-wheel-drive truck in the middle of East Los Angeles! With four kids and two frightened parents, we faced one of the greatest physical risks to our lives.

Lance Anderson—"Come on down to our place!"

Once again the Lord intervened by sending us some Adventist people who lived down in the valley. Betty Anderson was a wonderful person who understood country living and had come up to visit us before. Being a single mother with two sons, she too had considered settling on the mountain because of "the school." The promises of "true education" had attracted her earlier, but she changed her mind after seeing what our family experienced. We believe that God performed a miracle when Betty's son Lance arrived one freezing day. Although the roads were impassable, he decided to come up to see if we were alright. An expert driver under those conditions, he navigated the roads successfully.

Lance talked with my parents about our situation. As they sat near the wood stove, he assured them that everything would work out in the end. It was hard to believe that so much could have happened in such a short amount of time. We then prayed together and asked God to intervene in the situation. After that prayer Lance announced, "Come on down and stay with us in the valley until things work out for you." The next day he helped our family limp down 40 miles of treacherous icy mountain roads into the town of Covelo. It required several more trips up and down the mountain to get all our things moved.

The Adventist church in little Round Valley opened their arms to us and finally we once more felt the joys of the "first love" we had experienced after our baptism. My parents bought a little house on the Pomo Native Reservation in the valley. Among God's people again, we knew we were welcome there.

When the independent ministry from Los Angeles heard that we were now living in Covelo, some stopped by to see us. This time Mom had the intestinal fortitude to state firmly that we were no longer interested in their painful rules. We had been through enough and now desired to rejoice in a relationship with Christ. She lovingly and respectfully asked that they not visit or send any more publications. That major nightmare at last came to an end. Our journey with Jesus began again in earnest.

Gerry chose to remain in Los Angeles, and Louie took off for Mexico the next school year to take his first year of high school at Montemorelos College. I went for a short time to the little Covelo Adventist School, a one-room country schoolhouse with eight children that year. Mrs. Dishman was a wonderful teacher. She taught me about the value of responsibility in my school work by helping me through my struggles with homework.

Mrs. Dishman took personal time for me. She had a special quality about her that convinces a student that he or she is important and valuable. During the short time I spent there Mrs. Dishman taught me that God had a plan for my life. Although we could not discern that plan at the time, she said God would reveal it as life unfolded. I will always remember that woman, a symbol of the kind of mentors God would send throughout the rest of my life. When we walk with the Lord, He provides much more than we could ever think to ask for. My church school teacher was the evidence of things to come, people who would invest in me as a person in the name of Christ.

I also made a lifelong friend in Covelo named Tom Kruger. As we sat in that little school house together for the short time I lived there, we formed a bond that has endured for the past nearly three decades. Tom is a wonderful person with deep country roots and a savvy for people and their needs. To this day, he is like an extended member of the family.

The next school year, my freshman year of high school, I accompanied Louie to Montemorelos, Mexico. The college there is a great school. Students come from many countries and study a wide variety of courses. You can begin there in elementary school and continue on to complete degrees in many areas. A large number of students from the United States attended Montemorelos.

My brother Louie was popular on campus and had many friends. I began to meet them and compared them to what he had said about them when he called or wrote home the year before. It seemed that everyone knew and loved Louie. Proud of him, I have since sought to learn from his success.

Montemorelos is known for its incredible oranges. It has the largest navel oranges I have ever seen. You can easily get sick your first week there from eating too many of them. Immediately I began to make friends and to hang out with them during classes and church services. I joined a quartet and, with my newly changed voice, sang the bass part for the group. We sang often in the tile-floored hallways of the boy's dorm. I had a job with the grounds team, raking and trimming shrubs and playing marbles, the campus national sport, when the boss was not around.

One day a few students from Mexico City approached me on campus. One of them asked why I had so much money and then said that I had an obligation to share my money and belongings with them. It shocked me. Didn't they know that I too was poor? The issue later centered more on the fact that I was from the United States. Somehow, they perceived me as an outsider, which was something that I had not expected.

Little incidents continued on campus and I overheard occasional comments about me having lots of money. One day some guys confronted me and insisted that I was some kind of traitor. When I proudly announced that I was a Mexican, they quickly replied that I wasn't. Their discovery that I had been born in Los Angeles they saw as further evidence that I was not a Mexican. They clung to the belief that I was to blame for some kind of betrayal of my homeland. But how could I have chosen where to be born?

Throughout my childhood and into puberty I had struggled to find my identity. Back home in the United States people bluntly told me that I was not an American. Now others told me with the same conviction that I was not a Mexican. Who was I? When both countries used the term *alien* to describe me, I finally developed the idea that I was indeed some kind of little green being from another planet. Now, as I searched for my identity, no one knew how to help me and much less where to take me.

Just as in my earlier childhood, people gathered around occasionally to hear me speak Spanish in which I now had developed a slight English accent. People in Mexico expected me to speak perfect Spanish, just as in the United States they expected perfect English. I had to know who all the famous people were in Mexico with the same ease that I needed to know who all the famous men and women were in the United States. I had to be aware that I was "allowed" to live in Mexico just as I needed to be aware that I was "allowed" to live in the United States. Each country seemed to take it for granted that the other country claimed me.

God used this important time in my life as a preparation for my future. I now know that we cannot contribute anything in life if we do not know who we are. If I know who I am, then I have something to give to others. The whole issue was a loose end from my childhood and God wanted me to confront it head-on. The answer would further develop in my life during the next year and a half.

In the meantime I became sick with infectious hepatitis. I had a particularly bad case. I spent several days in the classroom and in my dorm room not knowing that I was sick. By the time my roommates carried me to the hospital, I had lost about 20 pounds and resembled a Halloween skeleton. One particular memory I have about hepatitis is that it really hurts. Your liver becomes inflamed, and you turn a bright-yellow color. I remember glancing into the mirror and seeing my bright yellow eyes and skin, wondering if I would ever again look the healthy shade of brown that I had enjoyed.

It turned out that we had a full-blown epidemic on campus. When I awoke at the hospital there were four other students there with hepatitis. All the patients were from the United States. To account for the fact that only Americans were sick, many students spread the rumor on campus that we had brought the disease from the U.S. Needless to say, we had fun speaking English across the hallways from our different rooms. Sitting in chairs at the doors of our rooms, we would shout across the hall. One of the more memorable practices in that hospital was the nightly back rubs that the nurses would give us. It intrigued me that the back rubs were part of the prescribed treatment for our condition—apparently as a favor from the doctor.

My brother Louie and my dorm roommates came to see me regularly. Louie really watched over me and once even sneaked in a banana, which I devoured even though I was on a restricted diet. Other friends came to see me also, but one particularly stood out. Her name was Sandra Escudero. Compassionate, she showed a genuine concern for my condition. As I think back on the experience, I remember the long conversations we had with her sitting on a chair in the hallway and me on a chair just inside my room. A large "Quarantine" sign on my door prohibited visitors from entering the room.

I looked forward to Sandra's visits. I had met her in classes and had come to feel special when in her presence. She took time for me in a way that no other girl had before. Asking nothing of me, she showed only true kindness. During the second week of my stay in the hospital, the school celebrated its yearly banquet. That banquet was the only major social event that allowed guys and girls to be together. And I was stuck in the hospital with a highly contagious disease!

The hospital was located on the north end of campus. I could hear lots of excitement across the grounds. Silently I watched the fireworks exploding outside my window and heard the festive music. The crowd of about 600 students and staff certainly enjoyed every part of the banquet. I realized that night that such social events actually meant something to me. I was growing up.

During the height of the festivities Sandra suddenly appeared. Quickly I wiped my face, hoping she hadn't noticed my glossy eyes. As if aware of my sorrow, she called me to the door and quietly handed me a flower from one of the tables at the banquet. I could see that she was taking a risk, because visiting hours were long past. We talked softly, and she wished me God's blessing. Finally, I rustled up the courage to tell her that, had I been able to, I would have asked her to go to the banquet with me. She smiled and after a moment disappeared down the dark hallway.

The next day a sudden and strong pain in my abdomen overwhelmed me. My dormitory dean walked into the room as nurses and doctors carried me to my bed. Witnessing the flurry of activity and the rush to start new IVs in my arms, he panicked. The dean ran back to the dorm and called my parents, saying that I was "gravely ill."

It was the worst news my parents could have received, since they were not sure what it meant. In my family the past two times we had heard those very words were because my grandparents had already died. It was the way my extended family uses to get us to go quickly to the site of a death in the family. My parents tearfully gathered some money together, and my mom left on the first plane out of San Francisco. The next morning when she walked into my room I almost literally melted with joy.

When the doctor appeared next, I realized that they had made arrangements for me to leave. We spent the rest of that day at the home of one of the school's professors. I was not ready for travel, but there seemed to be a rush to get me out quickly. At first light my mother and I were on a bus headed for the city of Monterrey, Mexico. There we boarded a plane bound for the United States. By that night I was home. As I left the plane and descended the steps, I now understood how other people feel when they return to their country. Kneeling, I reverently touched the warm California ground. The familiar soil almost smelled like a rustic perfume. It was as if I had closed my eyes and clicked my heels saying, "There's no place like home, there's no place like home . . ."

During the drive home I thought of Sandra. I did not have any opportunity to say farewell to her, and felt a terrible emptiness inside. My first experience of feelings for a girl had ended suddenly and out of my control. A large and unresolved void remained in my heart. Years later I learned that when Sandra walked cheerfully down the hallway and peered into my hospital room the next day, she found it sanitized and empty, with my bed neatly made. The chairs were now silent witnesses to my departure. She was saddened to learn that I had left. I would not get to see her again for 20 years.

As I look back at this point in my life, it is as if a graduation of sorts was occuring. The few months that I spent at Montemorelos helped me to learn that puberty is a time of opportunity in a person's life. As the body begins to change, so also the mind can begin to grasp things that were not as clear in the past. Puberty need not be an excuse for chaos, but it can instead be the golden transition into maturity. I began to make an inventory of my experiences and wanted to stop being a victim. I was tired of reacting to life as a *survivor*. Now I wanted to learn how to be a *surmounter*. The dynamic difference between simply surviving and victorious living is a wonderful attitude that we can develop through God's leading.

In a special way the Lord had prepared me for the calling He would extend to me. I had been baptized at the age of 10, just in time to preserve me from the street violence my brother Gerry now faced. Although I still deeply admired him, an unseen Power had protected me when confronted by the many temptations that I faced as I hung out with him in the neighborhood. I was able to refuse the drugs and alcohol through a strength that comes only from God. By God's grace I was now making positive choices.

At last I was ready to confront the issues of who I was as a person and what I was as a Christian. All the pain and insecurity of my childhood and all the victories in my life to that point were now ready to blossom into a true purpose under God. I had learned tremendous things from the Bible and from the writings of Ellen White. In my head I had gathered lots of information regarding doctrine, beliefs, and commitments. Now my growth would accelerate as never before in my life as God sent mentors into my life as never before.

I must state clearly that Jesus is my ultimate mentor. He is the hope of everything I want to be. Christ is the only true example for all of us. So when I refer to mentors in this book, I am talking about the people who demonstrate to me what Jesus is doing in them. Once I heard an inspired thought that now drives my being: "People develop methods; God develops people. People are God's method."

Consecrated people became an important tool in God's hand. Mentors have walked with me, prayed with me, studied Scripture with me, and faithfully shared their testimonies in Christ. From them I have unraveled the mysteries of life in Christ. A life that goes beyond mere passive beliefs and debates, but one that provokes active leadership in Christ and for Christ in the whole community.

CHAPTER THREE

"YOU'RE LATINO, 'MIJO'"

About 5:00, under a cool late-afternoon sun, we drove onto a street lined by tall pine trees. As we approached the gate, a kind man in the booth waved us into the beautiful Monterey Bay Academy campus. About six miles out of Watsonville, California, the school sprawls on gentle sloping land made up of some of the richest black farm soil I have ever seen. Lush fields of strawberries, raspberries, and other crops border the deep green lawns. The campus slopes downhill to a dramatic bluff that drops off like a 60-foot wall onto the shore of the Pacific Ocean, within the world-renowned Monterey Bay.

We reached a point in the drive that veered to the right up a hill to the main campus. As we crested the steep driveway, the view of the campus buildings opened before us. A cafeteria separated two beautiful dormitories on the right and a long administration building and other facilities spread downhill to the left. Faculty homes dotted the perimeter of the large campus. Pine and eucalyptus trees dominate the serene landscape. As we climbed out of the van, the deep roar of the water on the beach nearby testified elegantly to the beauty of the place.

It was mid-June 1975, and the school year had just ended the week before. My parents said that the students standing around in front of both dorms were staying at the school, working to earn their tuition for the next school year. The young people had just finished their workday and had freshened up

43

for supper. MBA hosted a variety of work opportunities, including two furniture mills, a candle factory, dairy, farm, laundry, and other jobs at about $2.10 an hour, top dollar for students that year!

My dad announced that he wanted Louie and I to stay and work there for the summer. The news caught me off guard. Louie asked a lot of questions and seemed to be excited about the prospect. I wasn't so sure. We walked down the hill into the administration building and met with John Eggers, the faculty member who led the student industry program. Mr. Eggers assured Dad that it would be a good move for us. At one point, he turned to Louie and me and said, "Well, I've got jobs for both you guys if you want 'em." Since Louie was tall, with big arms, Eggers offered him a job at the furniture mill. I was a lot shorter, with skinnier arms, and received a job at the candle factory. That very day Louie unpacked his things and moved into the boy's dorm at the school. Needing more time, however, I returned home with my parents to think it over.

The Utecht family of Ukiah, California, who had told us about the school, were excited about the fact that Louie was already there and that I might attend. Kenny, their son, succeeded in convincing me that we would have the time of our lives at MBA. The next week he and I joined Louie to earn money for the next school year.

Kenny was a gifted musician and quickly became a wonderful friend. We roomed together our first year there, and shared a passion for music that seemed to increase by the day. I had not had much experience performing in public, while Kenny had for years joined his sisters and other family members either playing his saxophone or singing with his powerful tenor voice.

I had been attempting to learn the guitar for some time and enjoyed strumming my little Harmony guitar that I had purchased at a store called Thrifty's. The guitar had been on sale, and I bought the instrument (actually, my parents did) for $9. My sister Martha and I had sung a few times in church, using that guitar to play our accompaniment. Although more of a toy, it became a symbol of my passion for music. I could actually pull organized notes from a guitar that hurt my fingers, had a tinny sound, and never quite stayed in tune. I guess it was not so much my style of playing, but the passion with which I learned to sing. One day I realized that people seemed more moved by my intensity in singing rather than my style or quality of intonation.

Really believing in what I sing, I don't care for entertainment when it comes to gospel music. Instead, I feel that music is a ministry that communicates God's love just as a sermon does.

Kenny and I soon began to sing together for various church ministries and, without my realizing it, he was helping me to develop a comfort that would follow me to this day. "Don't be scared, José," Kenny would tell me, assuring me that if God called me to sing, He would also give me the guts to do it. Kenny would say it because I usually got extremely nauseated on the days that we presented music to an audience.

But Kenny was right. I was now formally introduced and confirmed in the gift of public ministry. We would pray before all presentations and, even though we were nervous, we would walk onto the platform with confidence. The Lord blessed mightily. Through Kenny, God taught me an important lesson in leadership: if the Lord has called you, do not be afraid to take your gift to the people!

Johnny Perez—"It starts here, dude."

That summer at MBA I met Johnny Perez, a tough guy from Farmersville, a small agricultural town in the Central Valley of California. Although his town was tiny, it still had a gang problem among its youth. Johnny had just graduated with the class of 1975 and was working that summer to pay off his school bill. I had deep respect for him because he was the "lizard," the gang nickname he had earned on the streets. It gave him status in my estimation. He had earned his way to being a *veterano,* a title given to gang members who no longer have anything to prove, meaning that they are established.

What was most disarming about Johnny was his personality. He had become a gentle, loving guy who reached out to me with complete acceptance, much like my brother Gerry, with a cool Chicano attitude. Soon I noticed that Johnny took special time for me. He always talked to me as if I were his little brother.

That summer was so meaningful and so much fun that it raced by. Before I knew it, the school year had begun, and we had about 500 students register on the first day of school. The campus resembled an anthill with people all over the place!

As I met many new students, it surprised me at how geographically diverse the student body was. People came from all over California and beyond. I recall my first plunge into the crowd down at the get-acquainted activities on the beach. Instinctively I retreated into my usual shy exterior.

Many of the students frightened me. A large proportion of them came from wealthy families, something I was not accustomed to on such a large scale. Although there were plenty of us more needy students there, we easily disappeared amid the designer clothing on the beach.

Soon I turned 16 and was well into my sophomore year. As a teenager I had heard that young people were getting worse and worse, and indeed many reports in the media and in the church justified that viewpoint. But I was still one of those "neutral" students on campus and came to be labeled as "the most quiet person" in the sophomore class. In those days many considered long hair on men as "sinful," so I kept my hair as long as I could get away with without the dean calling me on it.

One night as I sat cross-legged in the hall of the dorm playing my little guitar, a couple guys walked by who said they played. Bart Vogel and John Vigil ran back to their rooms and soon returned with their guitars. That night I experienced my first jam session with fellow guitarists. As we played together, I noticed John doing something on his guitar and asked him to show me how to do it on mine. Similarly with Bart, I would inquire, "How did you do that?" They did the same about "my stuff," and we all began to grow quickly in our guitar skills. "Jamming" in the halls of a dormitory is one of the fastest ways to learn the guitar! John and Bart and I became fast friends as they lived their faith with me through the thick and thin of high school life. Bart's parents, Dolly and Howard, who always took time to love me, also did much to help me experience the beauty of a God who has a plan for my life.

We often spent Sundays playing for as long as seven hours and our fingers would ache afterward. The experience of playing music together led us to experiment with writing our own music. Soon all of us composed songs that we presented for different student programs.

On a particularly warm Sunday morning after breakfast, as I walked back to the dorm with guitars on my mind, I suddenly heard the sounds of thousands of birds. As I glanced at the sky, a beehive-shaped cloud of noisy migrating blackbirds bobbed and dipped across campus. Absorbed in watching them, I suddenly felt a tap on my shoulder. It was Johnny Perez.

Visiting the campus for the weekend, he had come to look me up to hang out for a while. As we stood together watching the birds, he began to talk about his experience in Christ. Although Johnny was not sophisticated by traditional definitions, his life spoke of the sophisticated influence of the Holy Spirit deep in his soul. We talked all morning as he testified to what God had done in his life since he had surrendered himself completely to Jesus.

Then he turned to me and said, "It starts here, dude." I stood silently as Johnny invited me to join him in dedicating my life to Christ. Instinctively I reminded him that I was already baptized, and he agreed that my baptism had been an important step. But he explained that I could now move further in committing my life to God. Johnny added that if I was going to do true ministry and have something real to share, it all started with this most basic of all commitments, a dedication of life itself to God, what inspired writers have referred to as "conversion." We inched back to the dorm and went to my room.

I will always treasure the memory of that day as we knelt in Room 232 on the top south hall of the boy's dorm. Johnny and I prayed a prayer, which in its simplicity, brought out my deepest commitment in life. Jesus became my Lord and Saviour that spring day in 1976.

Although my testimony may resemble many other stories offered as evidence of God's power to change lives, I am still dumbfounded by what this experience in Christ did for me. Giving my life to Jesus is something that I had heard about for a long time. I had thought that it consisted of merely holding on to certain beliefs and behaviors. But I soon discovered that Jesus is the experience that not only affects our lives but also those of others around us. From that day onward, I have learned that to live for Jesus is to share Him as never before.

The very week after I gave my life to Christ I received an invitation to join a student group that presented programs in area churches on behalf of the school. One day not long after that, as our group visited the Selma, California, Seventh-day Adventist Church, our program ended early. The pastor suddenly realized that he had almost a half hour of church service left! After an awkward silence, the pastor, scanning the front pew of nervous students, suddenly invited *me* to finish the program! "You guys ended a whole half hour early," he whispered in my ear. "You're going to have to get up and preach!"

Stunned, I felt my knees shake with fear and felt sick to my stomach. I hesitated for what seemed like seven seconds—a very long time when you're afraid! Then I went to that pulpit and preached about the final scenes of the crucifixion. The depictions of our Saviour's suffering in that unprepared sermon visibly wrenched the congregation at times. As I presented those gruesome events, the congregation obviously felt uncomfortable as they almost literally watched Jesus die before them. But I had no way of sanitizing the cruel reality of the penalty Christ bore for our sins.

In hindsight, I now realize just how blunt and plain the sermon had been. From that day forward, however, I have continued to intentionally take people past the cross in my sermons, no matter what the topic is. This experience occurred long before I knew that I would someday study for the ministry. At the age of 16 I preached my first official sermon, though I was sick with the nausea of stage fright for the rest of the day.

As the summer approached, a literature evangelist named David Lewis invited me to participate in a program called Community Crusade Against Drugs in the city of San Francisco. Although I was still only 16, my parents gave permission for me to join the team of students far from home. We worked directly on the streets of the city going door-to-door, presenting a message of drug-free living in the name of Jesus.

That summer was my first shot at bachelor life as well. My friends tell me I have never been the same since. I witnessed a whole world of people dying anonymously in their sins. But each of these people living deep in the cities of the world are still wonderful humans who need someone to love them. At the same time I remembered the many who die anonymously each day in Los Angeles. Those inner-city people, who some irreverently refer to as "the scum of the earth," are souls for whom

Christ willingly gave His life. My experience that summer profoundly shaped the intensity of my outlook on life and my zeal for the gospel ministry. Working on Dave's team in San Francisco pushed me into a Christianity that constantly seeks to make things happen in the community. The Lord also taught me to be faithful in the simple tasks of serving others.

One morning during our breakfast, the phone rang at the Spanish church where I lived with my roommate. The call was from the University of California Medical Center across the peninsula on the other side of San Francisco. A nurse at the other end of the line said that a woman was going to have serious surgery. The patient was a Seventh-day Adventist and was not from the area. The caller hoped that an Adventist pastor could visit the woman before her operation the next day.

I explained that our church pastor spoke no English and that it would be better if the pastor from the English-speaking church visited her. After giving the phone number of the San Francisco Tabernacle church, my roommate and I finished breakfast and prepared for the day's activities on the streets of the city.

I also hurriedly finished reading a favorite book that morning. Entitled *Field Guide to Wilderness Living,* it was a collection of tips for living in the harshest of wilderness conditions. I had loved the book so much that I had it hard bound. Now I took it with me in the car as we drove through San Francisco.

That night after we dropped off the last student team member, my roommate and I went to a fast-food restaurant on the corner of Market and Seventh streets. The time was about 11:30 p.m., and we sat quietly at the table. Suddenly, it hit us both at the same moment. With a sense of certainty we both exclaimed, "No one went to see that lady at the hospital today!" We could not say how we knew it. We simply felt sure that the hospital probably did not reach anyone to visit the woman facing serious surgery the next morning.

Quickly we picked up our food and ran out to the car. The drive across San Francisco is like no other trip in the world. As you climb the city's many hills you often have to stop on inclines that feel more like a wall than a street. Finally we reached the hospital and parked a block away, for even at that hour parking is scarce.

The hospital is a huge structure with many departments and patient floors. Yet with confidence we went directly to the ninth floor. When we emerged from the elevator the hallway was long and dark. Perhaps a 100 feet down the hall, a small light lit the nurses' station. Two small worried heads peered cautiously in our direction as we walked down the hallway. My roommate's rubber thongs slapped against the bottom of his feet and our bell-bottom pants matched our long shoulder-length hair, forming a silhouette that obviously frightened the nurses at that hour of the night.

The nurses called security, but it was too late. By then we stood before them, smiling and asking for a favor. I stated that we were "representing the Seventh-day Adventist Church" and had come to visit a patient who was having surgery in a few hours. The nurse reminded us that visiting hours had ended four hours earlier. But we insisted that our visit was pastoral and that we had to see the patient. One of the nurses finally said, "Well, I don't like this, but follow me, and I'll take you to her."

We followed her down the hall to a room where the nurse opened the door and let us in. To our amazement, we did indeed find that no one had come to see the patient. As we walked into the room it was exactly 12:00 midnight. A little night-light provided just enough light to see a woman sitting up in bed and in tears. "Don't tell me you're Adventists!" the woman exclaimed. We smiled and said that we were. "I had all but given up," she said, "but the Lord knew what He was going to do. At the stroke of midnight he has sent me two hippie Adventists to minister to me!"

It was the kind of experience I had read about in books. One of those miracle moments in the life of a Christian, as God meets someone's need through His people. We bonded almost immediately as the patient told us of her journey to that place. She stated that she now knew that she was ready for surgery since God had sent us to her. After that she led us in prayer and thanked God for the miracle of ministry that shows God cares and will not forsake us. Although we had gone to minister to her, instead she ministered to us. I learned that summer that this is the essence of ministry—freely you give, freely you receive.

After prayer the woman said, "My name is Catherine Gearing. Have you read my book *Field Guide to Wilderness*

Living?" My jaw must have dropped to the floor! It was my favorite book, the one I had just finished reading that very day! We spent the next hour rejoicing at how God demonstrates His love by bringing His people together. As we drove back across the peninsula that night, I held Catherine's book in my hands, knowing that we had done God's will in ministry. Catherine Gearing's surgery went very well the next day.

When I returned to school at the end of that summer I was a new person. What God did for me in San Francisco released me from the limitations I myself had set in my life through the years. All of us possess gifts that we have repressed because of different situations we have struggled with. But the Lord can break that hold and we can experience a fuller understanding of just how many things God has given us the capacity to do for Him and for His glory.

As soon as the new school year began, my parents surprised me with a new guitar! They had a few miraculous dollars that they used to buy a 12-string Brazilian instrument. If I indeed had now developed a ministry, they wanted to help me succeed. That Giannini Craviola guitar played for countless thousands of people around the world during the next 15 years, always in the context of a sermon.

I often think back to the day of those swarming blackbirds, and will always cherish that sunny day when I was 16. Little did I know that in giving my all to Jesus it would set off a virtual avalanche of growth in ministry. I am grateful to my friend Johnny Perez, who was faithful and persistent with me until I saw the light. Johnny took me from merely adhering to 27 beliefs to a dynamic lifestyle with Jesus Christ that is understood in 27 fundamental ways. I shifted from the "quiet" student on campus to a student with an attitude—an attitude for Jesus.

Josue and Ruth Rosado—"You're Latino, 'mijo.'"

Life at Monterey Bay Academy also taught me about the joy of successful cross-cultural existence. When my family left Louie and me at MBA, my parents went to see a special couple with a simple request. My dad, following a Mexican tradition, said to Josue and Ruth Rosado, *"Les encomiendo a mis hijos* [I commend my sons to you]." In other words, my parents were entrusting their two sons to the Rosado family's care.

The Rosados, a young Puerto Rican couple teaching at the academy at the time, pursued a vision of developing in Latino students a pride for their cultural and personal identity as an important basis for their giving back to society and the church. With their three little children, Leticia, Andrea, and Josueito, they responded to my parent's request and mentored us with a deep bond of caring. It was as if Josh and Ruth took us and a number of other Latino students into their home as a home-away-from-home.

About 15 Latino students registered that year at MBA and the Rosados loved us like their own kids. Josh established the "Spanish Seminar" in which we formed a student troupe that traveled throughout California presenting Spanish-language programs at Latino church services and youth rallies. I was one of the musicians and Louie served as one of the preachers for the group. Our mission was to emphasize Christian education and its benefits for Latino youth.

Ministry became even more priceless because we now experienced leadership in the context of our Latino heritage. Some of the most important moments for me occurred as we traveled from place to place. During the long road trips we had lots of time to talk with Josh as he drove the van. We would analyze what had happened in the churches we visited and then draw lessons for life from each experience. Also we could talk about topics that were important to us, such as relationships with the opposite gender, self-esteem, and other critical issues of adolescent life. Our discussions were in Spanish, in English, or in "Spanglish," depending on the moment.

Josh and Ruth led me to a fuller understanding of who I am. The previous years of confusion about my identity reached a turning point when, on one of our trips, I simply asked Josh to "tell me who I am." Without hesitation, he turned and said, "You're Latino, *mijo*."

"But if I'm Latino," I quickly responded, "aren't I also an American?"

"That's right," he added, "you're a Mexican-American, and you can be proud of that." He paused, then added, "And don't ever let anyone tell you differently."

I stared quietly out the window of the van as we drove another few miles. Amid the noise of the van on that dark road, I replayed the roar of the years of uncertainty about my cultural heritage. So many had told me that I was not American while others told me I was not Mexican. I could hardly believe that the answer was so simple . . . I was both!

Sensing that something important was happening inside me, Josh reached across and placed his strong hand on my shoulder. In a gentle, soft tone he informed me that I could take joyful pride in the Mexican traditions of my family and still be proud of my American flag. Indeed, this is America, a nation of peoples from all around the world. Although the blight of injustice still survived among us, I could best respond by first clinging to that which God had given me—my Mexican-American heritage!

Josh reminded me that California had been part of Mexico just a little more than a century before. My Native American roots, which give me my rich brown skin color, combined with the Spaniards, who had bequeathed me my facial hair and language. People can debate endlessly about the good and the evil involved in the development of the United States, but one thing became abundantly clear: we are all here now—we are *all* Americans.

The Rosados taught me that we can, with God's grace, live out the beauty of the mosaic of our country. The best way to help someone who thinks that America is limited to one culture or another is to portray the beauty of our cultures before that person. And the best person that we can be is to be who God made us. And when we can be who we are with Jesus in our lives, we become more effective in transforming the world than we ever thought possible.

Commander Leslie Goodwin—The incredible price of freedom

When I first entered history class, I could hear someone speaking a cockney English dialect. When I turned to see who was talking in a British accent, I saw Leslie Goodwin, a short man with a commanding presence. He is an amazing mixture of dignified, profoundly down-to-earth, and extremely funny. A group of students surrounded him, each looking at him with admiration. I soon discovered why they did.

History did not tend to be every student's favorite subject, but since school required it for graduation, everyone had to take it. I too entered the history classroom for the same reason. But as I listened to Leslie speak, my entire outlook began to change. In the first place, he used his cockney accent only when he wanted to make a point about his beloved England, the land of his birth and youth. The rest of the time he spoke in American English, his second of a dual citizenship. The man is brilliant and thinks quickly on his feet. I was fortunate to sit in the front row of his classroom.

Leslie's classroom made history an awesome venture into the past, one seen through the eyes of a biblical perspective. The course became an experience in a growing knowledge that God allows humans to lead on our planet. Sometimes we make mistakes and God can at times intervene to save us from ourselves. Goodwin examined historic events through a powerful narrative format. He compared them to parallels in biblical history and then used them as examples to challenge us today.

But that was not the most important part of experiencing Leslie Goodwin. By the time I had the privilege of sitting in his classroom I was 17. It had been an important age for Leslie. He had entered British military service during World War II with his identical twin brother, Norman, at that same age. That fact is what gives Leslie Goodwin the passion that he still possesses today.

Leslie had experienced the depths of war's incredible trauma. As a young man he lived in London during the Battle of Britain. Each night the Nazis sought to destroy England as a nation and eliminate the "British threat." To look into Leslie's eyes and realize that he could still see and hear the violence of battle as he told us of those terrible night air raids against London, awoke in me how God can use even trauma for our good. In story after story he told us of how God protected him from certain death. He even survived the sinking of his ship by a German U-boat.

The advantage that people who have been through chaos possess lies in God's power to take a painful experience and employ it for good. Many do not deal well with such experiences and may lead miserable lives afterward as a result. But when you have survived disaster with Christ, the experience becomes one of surmounting as well. You move from being "victim" to "victorious" in Jesus.

As Leslie talked of European history, his strength was his own experience and not a mere recitation of knowledge. When he would struggle to maintain composure as he shared a deeply personal experience, it demonstrated God's power again and again. Here was a man who has lived history and presented it with passion. He spoke from experience and understanding, not theory.

A reserve officer chaplain in the United States Coast Guard, Leslie sometimes wore his uniform in class because he had to attend to an assignment or event with the Coast Guard in the nearby town of Santa Cruz. The value of freedom is deeply ingrained in his life, the price of freedom clearly communicated through his experience.

I learned from Leslie Goodwin the value of my freedom in Christ and the price of that freedom through His experience on the cross for me. Also I discovered that history is a testimony of God's relationship with our planet and of our relationship with Him. In time I came to the powerful realization that history need not be something to which we are a victim. Instead, it is something that God wants to make through our lives!

Paul and Lynn Eagan—"The power of prayer"

During my sophomore year our Bible teacher suddenly left and Pastor Paul Eagan replaced him. With his wife, Lynn, and their two daughters, the young minister arrived to a challenging midterm classload that can frighten any new teacher.

Paul had been a pastor in the little church district of Orosi, California, and was experiencing his first plunge into teaching. Although not very tall, he is strong physically. Once he held up his 2-year-old daughter in class as she stood on his one hand!

Lynn, his bubbly and endearing wife, immediately bonded with us and made us feel like family. The Eagans at first struggled with the professional challenges of teaching, but that did not matter to us as students. We all knew that we could count on them for counseling on any issue, and confidentiality was guaranteed.

But an incredible spirit filled the Eagans in their ministry for the Lord. An aura of deep and unique love surrounded them with a profound intensity that I was not accustomed to. They also possessed a deep-seated and unshakable faith. Soon I discovered the incredible secret to their godliness.

Paul and Lynn prayed—prayed like no one I had ever met

before. Their prayers are actual, intentional communication with God. Beyond that, they couple their prayer life with a deep dedication to the study of Scripture. While the other Christians in my life also studied their Bibles, I found that the Eagans had an unusual faith in God that is contagious.

The prayers we had in class were an experience, not half-hearted formalities to begin or end a class session. When Paul Eagan prayed, it seemed that life stood still and God reached down to us. Class sessions were marked by commitment to the Word of God as our standard and then sealed with prayer.

On one occasion I called the Eagans about my desire to help a student struggling with a problem. After giving me sound advice, Paul said, "Let's pray about this, José."

"On the phone?" I asked.

"Right now, brother." Paul prayed for the student in a direct way, asking God to intervene with His will. Then he asked God to give me wisdom as I worked with the student. When I left the phone after that prayer, I experienced what Paul had prayed for. The student found resolution to his problem and I learned in new ways what God will do through the power of prayer.

The Eagans completely rely on biblical guidance for life. What some refer to as occasional "promises of Scripture" the Eagans consider indispensable tools for everyday living. Any personal notes I received from Paul would always contain a biblical nugget for the day. He would claim scriptural promises for me to encourage me, and thus succeeded in giving me a larger vision of ministry.

One day Paul had me paged during supper in the cafeteria. He sounded sober that evening as he informed me over the phone that the time had come to involve me in ministry for a specific student. The young person had dabbled in witchcraft for some time and was struggling against a kind of evil phenomenon. Paul mentioned that the student would stop by to talk with me later that evening. His counsel was that I pray with the student.

My heart, of course, stood still for a moment. I wasn't sure what to do under the circumstances. Paul assured me that the Lord had a plan and would be with me. After reviewing the passage of Scripture that confirms that "greater is He that is in me than he that is in the world," Paul then said, "Let's pray about this, José." Paul prayed. And again I sensed the Lord's presence in a simple way. We consecrated our lives to Christ and asked that the situation be resolved only according to His divine will.

When I returned to the dorm, the student in fact came to see me. We spent a few minutes talking and the student opened up about his desire to stop toying with evil. I could see that he had played with it for some time and was greatly shaken by his experience. Now he felt unable to stop and felt out of control both physically and spiritually.

My roommates arrived and I asked them to remain in the room with the student while I went to get something. I would take only a few minutes. But just as I reached the first floor of the dorm, I heard a piercing scream unlike anything that I had ever heard before. Almost immediately one of my roommates stood in front of me, telling me it was the student.

Racing back up the stairs, I followed the screams. As I reached my room, the door opened and the boy came out, deep panic in his eyes. I had never seen such fear, even on the face of a person facing death. He breathed deeply and foamed at the mouth. Although in a violent condition, he appeared to be trying to reach out to me as if wanting a hug, but something prevented him.

I happened to have my Bible in my hand, and in a loud voice I told him that I was going to pray in the name of Jesus. At that moment he seemed to be in pain and immediately ran around me down the hallway. All of this happened in a split second. I pursued him down the stairs and out the front door of the dormitory.

At that moment, Paul Eagan and a few other staff members, having heard the commotion, raced toward the dormitory porch. I reached the boy at the same moment that Paul did. Several of us grabbed the student and held him tightly. Paul led a simple and determined impromptu prayer. A prayer that we could hardly hear over the young man's screams. As we pronounced the name of Jesus in that prayer, he went limp in our arms.

We took him to the clinic on campus and noticed that he seemed completely drained of any strength. He needed cleaning and medical aid because he had shattered a window in my room with his fist and had cut himself badly in the forearm. That night I saw the power of prayer in new terms. Only 17 years old, I had never witnessed anything like this before. I realized that prayer, in the name of Jesus, will summon the power of heaven to the point that evil cannot resist and must flee.

The Lord also taught me something else that night. Such incidents cause a lot of panic. They can create an environment of great fear and trigger false revivals. Suddenly students began to fear that supernatural evil was invading the campus despite the fact that we had clear evidence of God's presence. Only one life had been affected in this way and then only because of his own choices. He was now resting quietly and rejoicing in the peace that comes from God. But it was hard to convince others that they had nothing to fear.

That night more than 20 students slept in my room. If you were to see the size of the room you would marvel at how that could be possible. Many students wanted to study the Bible and address spiritual issues in their lives. Others vowed to give up destructive habits and live new lives. I remember mentally sighing, not sure what to think about the motives behind such sudden conversions. Here were extremely frightened people searching nervously for a sense of security. It all seemed like a bad dream.

I learned that too often we look heavenward only out of fear. For some it is the emergency of a disaster or an accident. For others it is the onset of a dreaded disease. Whatever the cause, it is sad to realize that we seem to reserve prayer for emergencies, that we do not utilize the joyful experience of prayer as much as it could be. Thus many people stop praying the moment the fear subsides, having never learned the joy of daily communion with God.

The incident with the student that night frustrated me for some time. I would encounter similar phenomenon in other settings of ministry far from campus. What bothered me about such incidents was that I could not seem to communicate the peace and joy of serving Christ afterward. While there were powerful evidences of Jesus' power to deliver a person victimized by evil, I could not figure out an answer to the short-lived revivals that would follow.

Over time the Lord gave me the answer. Confronting such public displays of evil is not the strongest manifestation of prayer's power. After all, can it be hard for the Holy of holies to drive out evil? Is it difficult for Him who banished evil from heaven, and conquered evil once and for all on the cross, to free a soul in bondage? Studying further in the Bible and the writings of Ellen White, I set out to understand the role of healing and casting out of demons in the ministry of Jesus and His disciples. I had always understood that such phenomenon would appear at the end of time as one of the signs of God's work in His people. I found that it was indeed the case—but only when really necessary.

I discovered in my study that the devil actually used such incidents of possession to discredit Jesus' ministry, because they frightened people into repenting for the wrong reasons. Some Jewish leaders even argued that demon possession supported their accusation that He "cast out demons through the prince of demons." Even after He had dealt with demons and healed possibly thousands of people over a three-year span, many still demanded of Jesus, "Show us a sign!" I began to see why after healing someone Jesus often admonished the person to "tell no one" what had happened.

The experience of the prophet Elijah also fascinated me. Elijah had prayed and fire had fallen from heaven to prove that the God of Israel was the true God. But even after all that, we find through Elijah's experience that the power of God does not shine best through the earthquake, the wind, or the fire. Doing great physical phenomenon is easy for an omnipotent God. But God's power most clearly appears through the still small voice. The secret of God's power is that He is gentle and loving. People like to marvel at miracles and supernatural phenomenon, but nothing really impresses more than sinners who turn from death to life, because a loving God has invited them.

The Lord demonstrated that my prayer and Bible study provide the strongest opportunities for His power to save. In those moments I learned to go out of myself to pray for others with deeper conviction. Intercessory prayer became the single most decisive ministry that I can offer for another person. During the next few years I learned that to fast and pray privately for a soul in bondage is infinitely more powerful than publicly confronting evil.

I must point out that I am not saying that I am opposed to God's will occasionally calling for a public demonstration of His power. What I do mean, however, is that the greatest public demonstration of God's power appears in everyday people living a life with God in prayer . . . every day. It is a question of attitude. Prayer is the key.

As I came to understand the principles of the power of prayer, I have never again had to face the phenomenon of possession in public. God delivers people in His own way through the loving intercession of those who pray. We are told that prayer is "the key in the hand of faith to unlock heaven's storehouse." The Eagans helped me understand that key. I asked God to never let me lose that prayer key, because I could not imagine what life would be like if the doors to future growth in ministry were ever to remain closed!

CHAPTER FOUR

"GOD IS CALLING YOU TO BE A PASTOR"

M inistry was quickly becoming a major part of my life. By my senior year at Monterey Bay Academy, at age 18, I was traveling as many as three weekends a month to churches and schools throughout California. Our ministry involved concerts, preaching, and one-on-one contact with young people. Depending on the objectives for a trip, I traveled with Josh Rosado or Bart Vogel, John Vigil, Nancy Ortiz, and Kenny Utecht. Because each trip was different, so was each experience. That made each place we visited special and each ministry experience a unique blessing.

We also ministered in Hollister, California, with the school's student outreach teams every Tuesday night. Each week the MBA Greyhound buses left the campus with more than 50 students. After a 45 minute drive over the Pajaro Valley hills, we fanned out into the streets of Hollister. Some visited homes and met physical needs while others conducted home Bible study groups. My assignment involved leading a team that went door-to-door, singing with the guitar and bringing cheer to families. It initiated many Bible studies as the families we contacted sought answers to the challenges facing them.

God was accomplishing something that I never thought would happen. Doing the work of ministry was continually changing my outlook on life. My attitudes about my own life took on a new definition. For so long I had considered myself a "victim" of life's injustices and felt paralyzed to do anything about them. Now my life was redefining itself as I did everything possible to share what a liberating experience it is to have Jesus in my heart. I now prayed for the people who discriminated against me from time to time, because I was too focused to let them discourage me.

Ministry had altered both my tendency to be depressed over my sufferings as well as my outward commitment to relieving the suffering of others. Dr. Martin Luther King's words came to life. He had said that "you cannot drive out darkness with darkness; you need light to do that. You cannot drive out hate with hate; you need love to do that." The light of Jesus was dispelling even the darkest corners of my life.

Eliezer Benavides—"You have a destiny with the Lord."

One day while visiting the Mountain View Spanish church in the San Francisco Bay area, I met Pastor Eliezer Benavides. Our Latino student team was there to present the church service. Josh Rosado had introduced me to Pastor Benavides that morning with a recommendation that he talk to me about college. By now I had made many public statements that I was *not* going to college under any circumstances!

Pastor Benavides, who was also visiting the church that day, was the Spanish ministries coordinator for the Pacific Union Conference. The man was a legend, having been one of the pioneers of Latino ministries in North America for the Seventh-day Adventist Church. His mind functions like a computer, and he exhibited his gift long before computers were commonplace. Benavides' leadership has distinguished him for many years.

Sensing my hesitation when Rosado mentioned college, Pastor Benavides did not mention the subject of education during our first conversation. Instead, he asked me about the ministry that God was leading me in. It touched me that a man of such caliber in our denomination's leadership would take time for a teenager like me. I told him of the things that I was doing with Josh Rosado and my fellow ministry partners.

After we had visited for a while, Pastor Benavides told me that the amount of ministry occurring in my life deeply impressed him. Pointing out that I had no idea what God planned for my future, he challenged me always to do my best with whatever entered my life. "Pray and stay humble, and God will never fail you," he added. Then he asked if we could pray together. I quickly agreed, and with his hand on my shoulder, Pastor Benavides asked God to prepare me for whatever was to come in my life.

Not long afterward I graduated from academy. At that time I again stated that I was not going to college and instead went to Ukiah to launch "Rojas Upholstery and Vinyl Repair" with my parents. It deeply pained them that I did not want to go to college but they still supported me even if they didn't agree with my decision. The business opened, and we were off to a great start.

To make sure that my decision to stay out of college was final, I wrote to the state of California and rejected a large scholarship that it had granted to me just before graduation. In my mind I had taken the last step to make sure the "college thing" did not happen. Since it has a waiting list of literally thousands of worthy students, California automatically gives away unclaimed scholarships to others who more eagerly accept the privilege.

The Ukiah Seventh-day Adventist Church then appointed me associate personal ministries leader. The congregation, with more than 700 mostly professional members, asked me to conduct youth Bible studies and outreach. I now believed that I had made enough final commitments to satisfy everyone that I was not going to college. But the Lord still had another plan in mind. I did not know it at the time, but my parents still prayed almost daily that God would help me get to college. Nor did I know about the growing number of people who joined that prayer effort as time went on.

One day in December 1978 I received a letter from the state of California notifying me that I had to respond quickly to accept my scholarship. It shocked me, since I had already rejected that scholarship in writing six months earlier! My mom seized the moment and gently brought up the idea that "maybe God was telling me something." "Why else would there still be a scholarship on hold for you?" she asked meekly.

As if in a dream, I remember saying to her that I would agree to go to Pacific Union College only to "check things out." I dared not make a commitment for fear of increasing the pressure that I go to college. I thought that I could simply make a gesture and thus meet my obligation to have considered college and then resume my upholstery business. We closed the shop just after lunch that day and got into our van.

My mom and I drove the 80 miles south to PUC and arrived sometime in the early afternoon. We went to the counseling center and presented my state documents to them. Elinore Spoor, the director of the center, immediately stated that in all her years in education she had never seen anything like this occur. She had me take a test to see what my interests were. Within the hour my profile suggested that I "enjoy working in close proximity to people."

Then she sent me to PUC's Department of Education to interview with Penny Awn, who oversaw the early childhood education program. When Dr. Awn saw my documents she simply exclaimed, "God is calling you to college. We'll see you in a couple weeks for registration!"

The memory of the next few weeks is a blur to me. Before I knew it I was standing in line at PUC on registration day. As I went from station to station in the registration process, I was nervous because I did not know what to expect. I did not perceive myself as a student and could not imagine how things would go once I was immersed in college life.

I registered as an early childhood education major and was known as "the only man" in the program. I deeply enjoyed that study, however. My lab work was immensely enjoyable, as I worked directly with children. I learned to tell stories and to understand the developmental stages in the lives of children. It also intrigued me to learn that adults tend to be sophisticated expressions of what they were as children. The various stages of development in people's lives especially fascinated me, especially in how they shape the growth of faith.

Quickly, almost instinctively, I resumed my ministry activities also. Soon I traveled with groups to present concerts in churches and to preach. Also I went with Latino students using the same model that Josh Rosado had planted in my life. We would visit Latino churches and share Christ and the opportunities we had as Latinos to give back to our world through education. In addition, I joined an active Latino club on campus named "MEPE." It too ministered across the state in churches and for different events.

One day toward the end of the school year, a student approached me in the cafeteria. Pastor Weiland Wood of the Santa Rosa church had sent him to tell me of an opportunity for a Latino to give Bible studies in the town of Windsor, just outside of Healdsburg, California. The town was just over the mountains about 40 miles away.

My answer was immediate. I told the guy that I would not consider it, because "I was studying to be a teacher." The student assured me that it was only a summer job and that the Santa Rosa church would support me in anything I needed to advance Latino ministry in that town. He told me that a Schmidt family had worked for Latinos for three years and needed additional support. My no was final, and the student left me to finish my vegechick nuggets and tartar sauce.

The very next day, however, the cafeteria incident repeated itself, only more dramatically. Someone else approached my table while I was eating. As I stuffed a forkful of vegesausage and hash browns into my mouth, a shadow spread over my table. I looked up to see a large and imposing presence. Pastor Weiland Wood stood there with his two hands in semi-fists at his hips! "I have come all the way from the Santa Rosa church to see you!" he said. I sat up straight and don't know how I swallowed my food so quickly. With his chin held low and a smile on his face, he said, "So you think you don't want to come to Windsor, do you?" Rolling my tongue, in an effort to clear hash browns from my teeth, I stumbled a little as I answered, "I . . . I . . . I'm an education major. You really need to see one of the many theology majors here at the college."

Pastor Wood stood silently for a moment and looked right through me. I could immediately see that this man in his early 60s had vast experience in ministry and knew how to get things done. With a gentle and yet extremely firm voice he said, "Our church board voted to extend to you the invitation to work in Windsor this summer. Are you saying my board doesn't know what it is doing in God's work?" As I stared at him I suddenly realized that I did not know what to say. I could only look into his eyes and see a determined sincerity with a complete grasp of his goals as a pastor.

Faced with Pastor Wood's overwhelming conviction and purpose, I stood and extended my hand to him. After a final role of my tongue, I said, "When do I begin?"

He took my hand and pulled me close for a hug. "You won't regret your decision," he said. "God is doing something here. And He's going to use you to help us move it forward."

We agreed to meet the next week to make final arrangements. Then he left me alone to finish my meal, this time with a little heartburn. I also felt that familiar nausea of fear comparable to stage fright. Although I had by now done ministry in various communities for more than three years, I sensed that this was very different. I had conducted my previous ministry independently as a student. This offer had come as an official action of a large local church. They were going to trust me to carry out ministry as their representative in a town separate from the one where the church was located!

The day after school finished I met with Pastor Wood and discussed the summer ministry. The assignment was simple. Visiting interests in the town and conducting Bible studies, I would work closely with Sara Schmidt and her husband, complimenting their three years of Vacation Bible Schools and day camps. After a special moment of prayer in Pastor Wood's office, I left for Windsor.

That first Monday I stopped to see the Schmidts and prayed with them to ask God to pour out His Spirit on the task before us. By Monday afternoon I was walking the streets of Windsor and quickly found people with great needs. As I went from door to door, each home was different. Some lacked food, others jobs. Discouragement overwhelmed many, while still others tried to cope with children involved in gangs.

No matter what the situation, I felt comfortable because they were the issues of my own childhood. Since I kept in close touch with my brother Gerry in Los Angeles, I still harbored a love for the kids of the streets. Although I had been away from Los Angeles because of boarding school, my heart was still there in spirit through my cultural identity. At the end of the first day I had 11 people wanting Bible studies and had made commitments to help others with food and jobs.

By Wednesday I had 27 people launched in Bible studies and had brought food to many others. I realized that things were moving faster than I had imagined. And by the first Friday of my ministry assignment those 27 people had committed themselves to helping others who needed food and jobs. Suddenly we had a team of people who, brought together by the Gospel, now knew each other in a way they could never have before.

That Friday, as I drove past one of the two churches in town, an idea came to mind. The small Methodist church on the corner near the freeway was fully equipped with a sanctuary, classrooms, and fellowship hall. Going to the door, I knocked, hoping that someone would be there. After a moment the pastor, a young man on his first parish assignment, answered. Cautiously he stared at me. I looked every bit of my 19 years of age with a black mustache and my customary long straight hair below my shoulders.

When he asked if he could "help" me, I answered, "I hope you can!" I informed him that I was the student pastor of a new group of believers in town and that we would need a church to worship in on Saturdays. We are Seventh-day Adventists, I explained, seeking to meet Latino needs in town and be a part of faith community efforts to help others. The pastor, himself about 27 years old, appeared intrigued as he invited me into his office.

As we talked we immediately bonded. We had that fresh idealism that only comes from God. Then the Methodist pastor said, "I think that $300 will do it."

"Do what?" I asked, puzzled.

"The rent for the entire facility, including the sanctuary, the classrooms, and the fellowship hall." He added that he would of course have to take the request to his board, but that he did not expect any major problems. We shook hands on the deal and then prayed together as we began a new relationship in ministry.

When I walked out of the church that day I knew that the challenge would be to find the $300 a month to pay the rent. Returning to Santa Rosa, I met with Pastor Wood again. Seeing me, he asked, "Well, how did you enjoy your first week in Windsor?"

"The Lord has 27 people ready to meet for church next week," I reported, "and I have already shaken hands with the Methodist pastor for the use of his church. Can you give us $300 a month for the rent?"

Silence. Pastor Wood studied me to see if I was joking, but he sensed that I was serious. "Twenty-seven people are ready to meet?" he asked cautiously.

"They have all agreed to come to church since we have already launched Bible studies," I said. At that moment Pastor Wood pulled out his personal checkbook and wrote out a check to the Methodist church for our first month's rental payment. He said that he was going to have to "sell this to the board" but that he didn't think there would be a problem recovering his personal funds after the board voted to pay the Windsor rent.

As we both sat quietly in his office for a while we knew that the Lord was doing something special, something beyond the traditional definitions of ministry. Pastor Wood prayed with me and afterward said, "Isn't God wonderful?"

Swallowing a lump in my throat, I managed to whisper, "Yes, sir, He is."

The next Sabbath, my second week of ministry in Windsor, we celebrated our first official church service with an attendance of 32 people! My parents came to experience the service with me. After the sermon we enjoyed a wonderful potluck with an assortment of enchiladas, tacos, beans, rice, and other heavenly delicacies. The people were happy and enjoyed their first church service together.

After everyone had left, I entered the sanctuary alone and walked up to the front of the church. There I sat on the first pew, and in the silence of that place, began to cry. What was God doing? Why was I here? My 19-year-old heart trembled as I found myself technically "pastoring a church."

The responsibility weighed heavily on me as I thought of those God had entrusted to my leadership. As I now looked at a pulpit that was mine to watch over, I rose and went to the back of the sanctuary. There, as I knelt in prayer before Him, I asked God to be merciful with me, a sinner. I was keenly aware that the previous two weeks had been a huge risk for all the church leaders involved. Could they trust a teenager with the leadership of a new congregation?

That night I called Pastor Benavides. Deeply moved as I told him of the previous two weeks, he asked for a detailed report of each family. Then, in a moment that once again altered my life, Pastor Benavides said, "José, you must realize that God has called you to be a pastor. You have a destiny with the Lord." Admonishing me to be vigilant and always humble, he promised that "God would provide for the rest."

As the summer progressed, more people came, including several families from Santa Rosa. Larry and Maria Gibson attended faithfully. A successful stock broker, Larry gave me valuable financial advice on how to operate a church and taught me money management principles. Maria played the piano and led in other church functions. She became a trusted advisor and the elder of the church.

Another family that visited my little church were Jim and Sylvia Pappendick and their children. They immediately brought strong support and leadership. I noticed that Jim had a broad knowledge of church policy and would give me timely advice on issues as they would arise from time to time. One day, as I discussed a problem with him, I began to feel very much a failure. The stress of what I was doing was tremendous. I told him that I wanted some day to learn to be a leader in ministry but that I didn't think that I was able. "You're already leading," he said immediately. "Don't ever say that again."

When I asked him how he knew so much about ministry, he paused. I noticed that he was fighting tears. "I was a pastor for more than 14 years." That was almost equal to as long as I had been alive. Jim looked at me and told me that while he could not change what had happened in his life, he assured me that his heart remained in the gospel ministry. He took me under his wing as a mentor in ministry. Not long after that Jim gave me most of his ministerial library, including his notebooks from his masters of divinity courses at Andrews University.

Young and still committed to ministering to tough kids on the street, I also began an outreach for gang members in town. It turned out to be a wonderful addition to my Windsor ministry because it also helped some of the very families who were already attending. One day I went "cruising" with six "low rider" cars. We slowly drove around town, a ritual that parallels the strutting of a peacock. I drove a 1963 Volvo, fully restored and cut low with air shock absorbers. Other kids drove '63 Impalas and '55 Chevys. All cars were beautifully painted with true-spoke rims and hydraulic lift shock absorbers. The idea of cruising is to show your car to the community and publicly affirm your friendships. The kids could not believe that I would cruise with them since some Christians frown on the whole idea.

We reached a certain point in our drive and pulled over to

the side of the road. Everyone got out and spot-checked their cars to make sure every piece of chrome shone like a mirror. After that formality we gathered to talk as a group. This is usually the point where passersby can observe the cars and their drivers along the side of the road. All of it has deep meaning to the young people who do it. For me, it was a chance to talk about Jesus and the ultimate cruise we will have on the sea of glass.

Soon a police car arrived. As the officer got out of the vehicle I heard him call for backup as he prepared to confront "as many as 15 juveniles." Pulling his club from the backseat of the car, he slid it into the holder on his belt as he crossed the street. When he reached us he scanned the whole group, asking, "Any drugs today, gentlemen?" Two of the youth immediately began to protest, shouting, "We haven't done anything; why are you here?"

When the young people shifted a little, the officer reached for his club. As he unsnapped his gun holster, the officer nervously asked if we had "anything to hide." Immediately I said that everything was all right and that these young people were just out with me for a cruise. By now the officer was worried and responded that he needed more evidence that we indeed were "clean."

At that point one of the youth, who was attending my church, pointed to me as he said, "This is our pastor!" The officer looked at me with skepticism. His experience in law enforcement had taught him that when you confront a group of tough kids on the street, you can expect the unexpected. He said something to the effect of "Yeah, and my mom is Santa Claus." But when he saw a Bible in my hand, he paused. "Are you really a preacher?"

"Yes, I am," I replied.

"But how old are you?" When I told him I was 19, he could only shake his head in disbelief. Probably he had never encountered a young preacher among cruising low riders. Then he asked me what I was doing with a "crowd like this."

"Just loving kids, sir."

He nodded silently for a moment, then said, "All right, keep loving 'em."

As the officer turned to leave, he grabbed his walkie-talkie. We heard him cancel his request for backup as he walked to his car and drove away. At that point the youth cheered and said that I should go with them on more cruises in the future. We exchanged hugs and multistep handshakes in celebration. I reflected on the fact that these youth were accustomed to rejection and condemnation from society. What they did *not* expect was to simply be loved. The best way to disarm gang members is to love them. But it cannot be an occasional activity or event. It must come as a way of life, a long-term experience.

As the summer ended, the Northern California Conference asked me to continue serving as group leader of the Windsor Spanish church group. It granted me a small monthly stipend and I returned to PUC to begin a new major—theology. The Latino district pastor from St. Helena, California, Carlos Pidoux became my immediate supervisor under an arrangement with the Santa Rosa church. Throughout the next three and a half years of theology studies I would have my own church to lead. The incredible value of studying while at the same time pastoring still leaves me in awe today.

David Taylor—"Minorities can make it too."

My college experience had its challenges. My greatest fear was the idea that I could not survive college life. While I could easily manage the extracurricular activities, my studies were another matter. I struggled in Greek class and discovered that the class called Introduction to Theology was more like an introduction to pain.

Because my grade point average was 2.0 my first year, PUC put me on academic probation during the first quarter of the next year. Then my cumulative grade point average dropped further to 1.7. For those who are not sure what such numbers mean, they are the equivalent of failing grades. After that I received a "Dear José" letter from the admissions office explaining why I was no longer a student of the school and that if I wanted to return I needed to explain what I planned to do to remedy the situation.

At that point I felt that the bottom had fallen out and that maybe the Lord was about to lead me away from college. It was then that I met Dr. David Taylor, chair of the Theology Department. He had seen countless students in my predicament, and as an African-American, he had also witnessed many minority students give up on school because of their feelings of

71

failure and low self-esteem. He made it clear that he would not stand by and watch me self-destruct in my student life.

Without my knowing it, Dr. Taylor took me on as a special project among the many other students that he helped. He called me into his office to discuss what I planned to do to be readmitted. As we sat together, he reminded me that I could make it, but when he asked me why I was getting low grades, my answer was totally unexpected. "The reason why I'm getting lower grades is because I am a Mexican," I explained.

Dr. Taylor stared at me, not knowing whether to slap me or to cry. "What did you say?" I told him again that I believed that my low grades were due to my being Mexican. When he realized that I was serious, he asked, "Why?" I explained that a number of my elementary teachers had told me as a child that most Mexican children get lower grades and that I should not feel bad when it happened to me.

Leaning forward, he grabbed my forearm. "Listen, man, you have a brain like everybody else. Use it!" Then he added, "We minorities can make it too! What you need," he continued, "is to learn the skills of studying." We knelt and prayed there in his office. After that, Dr. Taylor wrote a letter to the admissions committee asking that I be readmitted and stating that he would take responsibility for helping me with my program.

Taylor had grown up in Camden, New Jersey, in a poor inner-city family with limited possibilities. Boxing on the tough streets had earned him the respect of others. Through Christ he had made a commitment to heaven, completed doctoral studies at Vanderbuilt University, and was now chairing the theology department at PUC.

Once again, another Black preacher was shaping my life. As with Dr. Martin Luther King, Jr., from whom I learned about personhood in the community, and Pastor Byron Spears, who had taught me about personhood in Jesus, now Dr. Taylor taught me about personhood as a student and spiritual leader for Christ.

Ruthie Perez—"If you ever need someone to talk to . . ."

During my first year at Pacific Union College I met a wonderful woman. Well, actually, she met me, or something to that effect. The college celebrated a special weekend each year called "reverse weekend." During it the girls asked the guys out to an assortment of planned events on campus. The young woman's name was Ruthie Perez.

I received a telephone call during the week before reverse weekend. When I answered I could hear a couple women talking in the background. Suddenly another woman said, "Here, give me the phone; I'll do it. Hi, my name is Ruthie Perez," she said abruptly. "I was wondering if you would like to go out with me to church vespers this Friday night." The others giggled behind her as Ruthie settled a dare and asked me out.

When I realized who was asking me out I nearly hit the floor. I had a concert out of town that weekend and could not accept. As we talked by phone I begged her for a "rain check." She agreed. The next week I asked to meet her at chapel services in the college church on Wednesday. The morning of chapel I wandered down to the church along with many other students, thinking of what I would say to her. All I knew was that she was one of the most beautiful women on campus and I felt that I would melt into a puddle when I met her.

As I walked into the large foyer of the college church I glanced around to see if Ruthie was already there. Suddenly I felt a tap on my shoulder. When I turned around, I looked into the beautiful eyes of a humble and caring person. Extending her hand and with a firm handshake, she said, "Hi, I'm Ruthie Perez." I, of course, melted into a puddle. Stumbling for words and struggling to remember my name, I incoherently said something to the effect of "I'm glad to meet you too."

After chapel that day I began to ask her out more formally. Both she and I had been dating others for a time and now enjoyed the opportunity of getting acquainted. We dated by going out to fast-food restaurants and the cafeteria as did other students whose money was tied up in tuition. Soon I discovered that Ruthie was an unusual person of deep-seated faith and compassion. She had a wonderful, gentle personality and always strived to serve people. Her eyes, as big as her heart, glowed with acceptance of others.

What is most disarming about Ruthie is her unassuming capacity to lead. While many do it through public display, Ruthie does virtually all of her leadership behind the scenes, out of public sight. Even from the first time I met her I discovered that she has a special gift for understanding human nature and a wisdom that far surpasses the average person. Ruthie can always see a situation differently than everyone else. Her counsel is something many people seek, and she always has time to listen to whoever is in need.

As time progressed, Ruthie and I became close. I still look today at the picture she dedicated to me at the end of the school year. It still encapsulates our relationship. "If you ever need someone to talk to, I am here," she wrote. Her dedication to God and people attracted me and won my heart. Ruthie became my best friend. I fell in love with the woman of my dreams.

Right after I launched the new little church in Windsor, Ruthie was there with me. Although she repeatedly reminded me that she "was not going to marry a minister," she stood by my side and worked closely with the church members. The people considered her their daughter, responding to her authentic love for their families.

After almost a year of dating, the day came when I asked Ruthie to marry me. When she said yes, my parents, according to old Mexican tradition, went to her parent's house in Stockton, California. After eating a nice meal, we all went into the Perez living room. Ruthie sat on one side of the room with her parents, and I sat nervously on the other side with mine. My dad made the speech to Ruthie's parents, affirming that their daughter and I loved each other and that they had come to request her hand for their son in marriage. Suddenly I felt weak as the thought hit me, *What if her parents say no?*

Estanislado and Maria Perez said the magic word yes. We discussed plans for the marriage and set a date for the wedding the next year. My ministry continued to take on new dynamics as Ruthie and I ministered together. At first she felt that she would never be a pastor's wife because she did not play the piano or have the ability to stand before a microphone. But while working with the congregation at Windsor, she found that people respected her gifts. Ruthie and I became a strong ministry team because she sings all the notes that I do not. Wherever I am weak, she is strong. We complement one another to the point that we found that we truly need each other. The Lord saw to that.

On September 7, 1980, when we were 20 years old, Ruthie

and I were married. Dr. David Taylor officiated at our wedding, and once again, he saw me through another important moment of my life. The English Oaks church in Lodi, California, was full of friends and relatives who came to celebrate our joy. On that day the woman of my dreams became the woman of my life.

CHAPTER FIVE

"BE AGGRESSIVE, GUY"

By the time I finished my fourth year at PUC I discovered that I did not have enough credits to graduate. My low grades during my first few quarters had taken their toll. Dr. Taylor called me in and we went over my transcript. Although I had made progress in my work, the failed courses needed to be repeated in order to meet all my degree requirements and raise my overall grade point average.

What hurt the most was that I did not even qualify to be interviewed by the conference presidents when they came to examine prospective pastors for their fields. I could only watch sadly as excited friends entered and exited the interview rooms. Dr. Taylor assured me that my day would come. I had to trust God.

Pacific Union College sent me a letter informing that they were prepared to readmit me the next school year. My problem was that I had depleted my major scholarships and Ruthie and I did not have enough money to remain in school. It was a very difficult time for us. My wife had put her own studies on hold so that I could finish my school work. The idea of leaving PUC before I completed a degree truly brought on a crisis. What were we to do? How could we continue to minister and make a living at the same time?

One week after the bad news regarding my studies, I received a phone call from Pastor Isaac Lara. As the Coordinator for Latino Ministries in the Central California Conference, he and I had met before. I had helped in a newly established Latino church in Wasco, California, the year before.

Pastor Lara offered me the opportunity to serve as the assistant pastor in the Fresno Spanish church district. He suggested that I could finish my studies by correspondence or through a future leave of absence. Ruthie and I now saw that the Lord was looking over us and continuing to guide our steps.

What touched me about Pastor Lara was his belief in us as a ministerial couple. He affirmed us and challenged us to continue growing in ministry. Ruthie and I prayed for two days, asking God to show us the way we should go. At the end of that time we felt convinced that He indeed wanted us to accept the Fresno position.

When I telephoned Pastor Lara to formally accept the offer, he told me that we had made the right decision. As Pastor Wood had stated four years earlier, now Pastor Lara repeated that "great things" were happening in Fresno and that God had a plan for us there.

The last thing that he said to me as we finished our conversation was "Be aggressive, guy." When I asked what he meant, he simply stated, "One of your gifts is a willingness to face great odds, so never give into fear, no matter what the circumstances!" Then he prayed with me. He asked God to keep me "aggressive" as our ministry moved into central California. We packed our things to begin our new ministry the very next week, on the first Sabbath of July 1982.

Fresno is a city in the middle of the agricultural and farm belt of California. Containing millions of acres of rich farm soil, the Central Valley of California produces literally every fruit, nut, and vegetable imaginable except for the most tropical products. It also hosts many dairies that provide a large proportion of California's milk. If California were to be a nation, it would be the seventh richest nation in the world, in large part because of its huge agricultural and farm assets.

The massive Sierra Nevadas shadow the Central Valley with

Sequoia and Yosemite national parks only a quick drive up the ridge. Yosemite National Park hosts the majesty of Half Dome and El Capitan, two of the largest single blocks of granite on earth. The General Grant in Sequoia National Park is one of the largest trees in the world.

As with most of California, a person can ski in deep snow at 10,000 feet, pick strawberries in the valley, and play on the beach, all on the same day! I had lived close to mountains all my life and had also lived near the beach for three years at Monterey Bay. It was to be my first experience in the "farm belt."

I thought I would feel out of place among the farms. After all, what was a "city boy" to do among fields and cows? But I found that the small towns of the Central Valley face some of the same challenges as the largest cities. It surprised me to learn that drug abuse and gang activity tend to be just as prevalent in small farm towns as they are in Los Angeles or San Francisco.

Eliseo Orozco—"Learn the lesson of loyalty."

When Ruthie and I arrived at the Fresno Spanish church on that warm Sabbath morning, the senior pastor, Eliseo Orozco, waited for us on the front porch. Pastor Lara had told him that "an aggressive young man" was coming to be his assistant pastor. When we drove up in a loud Chevy Camaro with low-profile tires and polished rims, he took a second look.

Wearing a neatly ironed black three-piece suit, I jumped out of the car and smiled at him saying, "Hi! You must be Pastor Orozco!" I could see him staring at my hair resting on my shoulders and glistening in the morning sunlight. As he paused on the steps before us I'm sure that a million thoughts must have crossed his mind when he realized that I was the long-awaited assistant pastor for his district.

Indeed, life doesn't always give us what we expect, but we can take courage in the conviction that God always provides what is best for the situation. The sight of Ruthie getting out of the car brought a needed balance to the moment. By then, Eliseo's wife, Priscilla, joined him. Together they warmly welcomed us to the church and introduced us to the congregation.

Working with Eliseo was my first experience as a formal employee of the church. The policies that govern pastors and their work relationships were more clearly drawn than in my previous labors in Windsor. I found early that I would have to learn how all of these relationships operated together for the smooth operation of ministry in a district.

Eliseo was wonderful to work for. He had also been raised in Los Angeles. I called my brother Gerry to tell him that I worked with a guy that looked just like him. Whenever I glanced at Eliseo, I really felt as if I was seeing Gerry! The chances of finding someone who actually resembles family is one in a million. But what made Eliseo the most fun was that we truly connected as colleagues and friends. I came to trust Eliseo with my life.

We led the Fresno church with its 220 members and a newly established group in the town of Madera to the north with about 100 members. I preached twice a week, conducted Bible studies, and visited homes with Eliseo. As we drove around town together, I saw in him a refined expertise in working with people. His years of ministry had taught him valuable lessons that he eagerly passed on to me.

After we would visit a home, we would return to the car and analyze what had happened. He helped me understand the many issues affecting human relationships or the lack thereof. Eliseo began to take my limitless energy and focus it methodically on specific goals in ministry. When I arrived in Fresno I probably could throw the equivalent of a "95-mph fastball" in ministry. Eliseo patiently taught me the equivalent of the "art of pitching"—everything from the "sinker" to the "curve," the "knuckleball," and the "change-up." My understanding and experience in ministry continued to broaden quickly under his mentorship.

This man was teaching me discipline. I'm sure that at times Eliseo wondered if I would ever fully mature. Being a mentor to young people is not always easy. But the rewards of faithful investments in them always last for generations to come. I thank God for Eliseo's patience, for through him God did do a marvelous thing. A major lesson was to come that would form another foundation in me for leadership.

Ministry requires a constant need to manage conflict. It appears that since churches consist of people, conflict is inevitable. While some churches succeed in limiting its damage, I have not yet seen a church that has totally eliminated it altogether. One of the easiest temptations facing pastors during such conflict is to allow their emotions to control the situation.

One day as we drove along Ashlan Avenue in Fresno, Eliseo turned to me and solemnly said, "An important issue for a leader is to learn the lesson of loyalty." I asked what he meant. "Loyalty is a deep commitment to a mission," he explained, adding, "When you see God leading a ministry, your responsibility is to see that ministry succeed." He explained to me how so often people do not understand what it means to be consistent in supporting leaders.

Not long afterward there arose a division in the church over one of our programs. Eliseo became a focus of attack from some of the members. I remember clearly how simple it was for me to stand by him. It was not a mere blind allegiance to a man. Rather, I had learned that loyalty shapes both the ministry and those called to carry it out. Some people seem to drift with the prevailing current when it comes to a program or a leader. But God showed me that to be loyal is a sacred responsibility.

One cannot overstate the issue of loyalty. One of the most dangerous problems that we face today as Christians is precisely a lack of loyalty. People who gossip demonstrate disloyalty to ministry by weakening those God has charged to carry out His work. When we are loyal we speak up on issues, we support people, we stand for the principles that make ministry happen.

While the concept is difficult to explain in words, it is easy to understand when you experience it. A leader who has not grasped the lesson of loyalty will always suffer unnecessarily and will often face confusion over objectives and goals. I learned with Eliseo that loyalty is a result of a committed leadership.

God blessed our work mightily. In the five years that we worked together, the Fresno Spanish church bought a large property and grew to more than 600 members. The new group that we planted in the town of Madera became a full church of more than 140 members within the first two years.

James Pimentel—"Focus and specialize."

Part of my work in Fresno included opportunities to participate in conference-wide events. One day, as we were planning a training program for lay members with a group of pastors, we arrived at the task of assigning pastors to teach the various courses. When the youth ministry course came up for discussion, we talked among ourselves who should lead that group. Rafael Perez, the pastor from the Dinuba Spanish church, said, "Let's put José in that role—he is a 'youth pastor.'"

I felt a chill go down my spine. Turning to him, I responded that I was a pastor in the district but not in "youth." Rafael looked directly at me as he rephrased his conviction. "Look around you when you minister and see how the youth are drawn to you. You behave as their leader. That is a youth pastor."

Not long after that our pastors also voted on assigning one of the Latino pastors to manage the conference-wide Latino youth congresses that occurred twice a year at Camp Wawona in Yosemite National Park. Once again Rafael urged that they select me because I was a "youth pastor." This time Jim Pimentel the conference associate youth director, was in the meeting. That day the pastors elected me with a strong vote of confidence. While I would still labor as a pastor in the Fresno Spanish District, I would also work for Latino youth throughout the conference.

I began to work with Jim Pimentel on a regular basis as we planned Latino youth events together. Soon he introduced me to the conference youth director, Richard Hamilton, and we kept him informed of all our activities. As in my experience with Eliseo, Jim took me into his confidence and treated me as a member of his team.

Pimentel took ministry seriously and mentored me through each experience. I noticed that he also meticulously analyzed each issue that would arise so that I learned the key points to repeat or avoid in the future. Although Jim provided supervision, he fully expected me to be in charge of the program. He assisted me with issues, but only enough to get me to flap my own wings and fly. I quickly learned about youth ministry.

One day the Lord confirmed within me the rewarding nature of working with youth. The response that He brought from youth and their parents through my ministry was undeniable. Later I went to see Jim about my growing conviction. When I spoke with him about it, he said, "You must now come to the point where you focus and specialize in ministry." Leaning toward me, he asked, "Do you want to go into youth ministry?" I replied that I did feel that God was calling me to it and that I wanted to grow further. Jim then advised me to see Richard Hamilton and share my conviction with him.

I made an appointment with Hamilton, and Jim helped me put my documents together, complete with a cover letter explaining my commitment. When the day arrived, I sat with Richard in his office and continually swallowed a big lump in my throat. I felt a cold sweat and worried about saying the wrong thing and being misunderstood.

Richard stood, walked around his desk to sit next to me, and asked, "What can I do for you?"

The first words that burst out were "I want to be just like you."

Smiling and nodding, he responded, "You want to go into youth ministry?" I assured him that I did and asked what I needed to do to accomplish that.

Richard wasted no time. "First, you don't need to be like me—be like Christ in working with youth. Second, go back to school and finish your degree." I sat up straight. I had forgotten about finishing my degree! "The Lord already has a plan for your ministry with youth," he continued, "but you must now go back to school and finish what you began." He advised me that true success was being faithful and that God would see me through the rest. But none of that would occur within the organized church if I didn't finish my degree. We prayed together as the meeting ended.

Jim was waiting for me and took me out to lunch. While we ate together he told me that he was proud of me, and that I could count on his help in continuing my growth in youth ministry. After lunch we went fishing along the foothills of the Sierras just outside of Madera. Later that week I received a letter from Jim affirming my work. At the end of it he said, "If we ever had the chance to work together for youth in a conference setting, I would greatly look forward to that day." I still take that letter out and read it from time to time.

Within two weeks Richard Hamilton sent me as the conference's official delegate to the Youth Specialties Convention in Portland, Oregon. After that day the conference Youth Department included me in its planning and activities. These men invested their time and resources to provide me the opportunity to grow in youth leadership. Eliseo kindly shared me during such occasions as long as I was still in his church district.

Jim and I worked with Rafael and established two Latino youth federations, one in the Valley and another in the San Francisco Bay area. Many youth joined, representing more than 30 churches. God blessed the efforts and the growth continued. I also began a dialogue with the conference about returning to school to finish my degree.

Another major lesson God taught me in the Central Valley involved another kind of leadership. Major humanitarian and social issues in our communities needed addressing, and I found that the church was in a unique position to do something about them. What was my role when people were hurting or discriminated against? Was I simply to turn and say that I would pray about it, or was God calling me to do something about humanitarian needs and social justice?

One day a bill in Congress called for a restructuring of immigration laws. Being of Mexican descent, I had been aware of the tension over this issue for many years, having been myself stopped by U.S. Immigration officials and asked for proof of citizenship. I grew up accustomed to such immigration restructuring proposals being floated every four years just before the U.S. presidential elections. It makes a good campaign issue that draws on the anger of voters. But what made that particular bill frightening was a provision that all Americans of Mexican descent would have to carry an ID card to prove that we were citizens.

Our congregations in Madera and Fresno consisted mostly of people of Mexican and Central American descent. Such a law limiting American rights to a narrow group of people, was indeed frightening. I prayed and asked God what I as a pastor could do. While we as a church take the position not to get involved in politics, I felt the bill struck at the heart of human dignity. I came to the clear conclusion that it involved not a political, but rather, a moral issue.

After consulting with others I confirmed that we as a church teach that someday government would move against us, favoring one group over another through the indignity of limiting the day of worship. I noticed that when a law affects our own rights it becomes very easy to know what to do. The immigration bill would affect a large proportion of Adventists as well as the state of California in general.

I made a difficult decision. After praying about it, I decided that I needed to get involved. I talked with city officials to ask them what they planned to do about the issue and also contacted our local congressional representative's office to express my congregation's concerns about the bill. Not long after that, as we were in the midst of the U.S. presidential campaign, I talked with several of the candidates who came through town. Attending their town hall meetings, I expressed our deep concerns to governmental officials, at the same time pushing them to make commitments in support of their citizens. We even took to the media and spoke out about the need for specific changes in the bill.

Through the leadership of Pastor John Stevens, then the director of public affairs and religious liberty for the Pacific Union Conference, I also talked briefly with the majority whip of the United States Senate and heard his assurances that some of the measure's provisions would be negotiated out of the bill in Congress.

The next month we celebrated the removal of the dangerous provision from the bill. After that experience I recognized that such things were also part of my responsibility in ministry. Never again have I confused moral issues with political issues. When something is right for humanity, it simply is the right thing to do. This is what Jesus did when He took moral positions in His ministry.

A few months later a major poultry processing plant in Fresno fired one of our deacons. The company refused to grant him Sabbath off so he could go to church, even though it had granted him the Sabbath for more than two years. A new supervisor simply no longer wanted to honor the previous agreement.

Our deacon even suffered financial reprisals from the company when he protested the injustice. No one had ever confronted this giant company before, and thus it felt safe. The young deacon had a wife and two small children at the time and faced immense need. The situation was critical for them.

Pastor Dick Fenn, then the assistant to the president for our conference, called me to discuss our "strategic response" to the situation. With Eliseo's blessing we met over supper at a restaurant. There we decided that the case clearly violated our deacon's rights at the company. We further made plans to file a complaint with the Fresno field office of the Equal Employment Opportunity Commission of the federal government.

Dick and I had to study the 1964 Civil Rights Act to understand the specific issues we needed to bring up at the hearing scheduled a month later. He had studied this law through his interest in religious liberty issues while I had examined the same law because of my concern about civil rights. On the day of the hearing, Dick and I arrived at the office and could see from the number of vehicles in the parking lot that we were in for problems. Before we got out of the car, we prayed, asking God to intervene in human affairs and make His will known. After prayer, Dick and I shook hands and said, "Let's go do this."

As we walked across the parking lot we saw two Rolls-Royces parked in the closest slots to the front door of the building. I swallowed hard as we walked by. Entering the building, we walked into a room with a long table. Ten people sat on one side and an arbiter occupied the end. The arbiter, a gentle and soft-spoken woman, smiled and said, "Welcome! Your place is on this side of table."

As Dick and I sat down we realized that we were in trouble. The team across the table from us introduced themselves. They had their plant supervisors and managers at the table, with additional representation from their administrative offices in Los Angeles. The room went cold when two of the people there introduced themselves as "the corporate attorneys" for the company. They were based in Beverly Hills, accounting for the Rolls-Royces outside.

Dick and I took deep breaths and stated that had we known that we could have had legal counsel present we would have brought our Adventist attorney, Claude Morgan, from Sacramento to be with us that day. The arbiter motioned that since we were already there that we needed to move forward with the proceeding. We agreed and the meeting got under way.

After a few remarks regarding ground rules from the arbiter, the lead attorney for the company began to say how it had done everything under the law to help the employee that they subsequently fired. He outlined the supposed steps taken, leading to the employee's dismissal. Then, turning to Dick and me, the attorney looked intently at us and said, "You cannot win this. It is impossible to prevail against us, because we have performed all appropriate steps to safeguard the rights of the fired employee."

I am not an attorney, but even I could see that the large team in front of us was attempting to intimidate us into a short meeting. Just to make sure that he had gotten his point across, the attorney added, "Don't even try to fight us . . . we will win." I fought the internal inclination to panic. We were clearly out of our league at that table.

The opposition had thrown us a powerful "bluff." All they could see were two pastors sitting meekly before them. But they made one major fundamental miscalculation. They did not know that we had prayed and given the issue to the Lord. In that moment I understood more clearly David's experience when he stood before Goliath. People may possess sophisticated tools and weapons, but there is something special about "coming in the name of the Lord." When something is God's will and His people have prayed and consecrated it to Him, it is the opposition that is in trouble.

I recalled the promise in Matthew 10:19, in which Jesus says, "Take no thought how or what ye shall speak: for it shall be given you in that hour what ye shall speak." In the book of Luke, Jesus adds: "For I will give you a mouth and wisdom, which all your advarsaries shall not be able to gainsay nor resist" (Luke 21:15). The next hour and a half demonstrated His promise to be absolutely true.

Dick began by laying out the premise of "reasonable accommodation" set out in the language of Title 7 of the Civil Rights Code. We tag-teamed to prove with meticulous detail how our young deacon had received letters of commendation from supervisors during the two years that the company had granted him Sabbath off. The work of the employee had been superior. Then we showed how granting the Sabbath did not in any way create any "reasonable hardship" for the company. Instead, we demonstrated how the company benefited by such a loyal and productive employee, who had also mentored new employees after being promoted to shift leader during that same period.

Finally we explained how the arrival of a new supervisor had ended everything. The new boss simply decided she didn't want to follow previous procedures and used the old and feeble argument that if she granted the Sabbath to this employee, soon everyone would want "a day off for everything from birthdays to church services." Further we showed how our deacon had offered to take a cut in pay and relinquish his shift leadership to make it easier for the company to give him the Sabbath. But all of it had been to no avail, and the deacon had lost his job, anyway.

Our presentation appeared to touch the arbiter, and she called for a break before proceeding any further. During the intermission one of the corporate attorneys approached me quietly and said, "Can we come to some kind of agreement on this? Maybe a money settlement can help end this stalemate."

"I don't see a stalemate," I replied, "merely a refusal by a large company to return a person to his rightful job with the back pay due him."

When we reassembled at the table, our demand was simple: "Give this man his job back." The arbiter asked a number of positive clarifying questions. The team on the other side of the table began to recognize that the arbiter was seeing our point of view as valid. I could sense the hand of God moving in our midst because much more than two hardheaded preachers was at work. God was confirming what happens when you are faithful in standing for justice in the lives of others. We ended the meeting with words of encouragement from the arbiter to continue our effort to settle among ourselves. In the meantime she would consider the arguments and issue a decision after a month.

Throughout the next month the company tried at different times to settle with money or to get us to permit a new "firing" of the employee and allow it to rehire him under a new policy. But we realized that if we accepted any new structure, our deacon would lose his rights, because he would have placed himself under new rules that did not protect him.

After the month had expired, the Equal Employment Opportunity Commission of the U.S. government found that the large poultry company had indeed violated the civil rights of our deacon and referred the case to the state office in San Francisco. The state office later ruled in favor of our deacon as well, and the case went to the national office of the Equal Employment Opportunity Commission in Washington, D.C. Incredibly, the national office also supported our deacon, and the United States government prepared to file a federal lawsuit against the poultry company for violating the civil rights of a quality employee.

The company quickly responded, offering our deacon his job back and completely restructuring their policies to grant any future employee, who can show conscientious belief, the right to worship on a specific day of the week. All the plants operated by the company, employing thousands of people across California, came under the new rules. Thus, countless others during the years since that time have received Sabbath accommodations.

The incident was my second experience working publicly with an issue of justice that affected the lives of many people. The Lord plainly showed me that ministry is not limited to the sanctuary and the planning committee. The most important ministry occurs in the community. It is in the community that others see and hear our beliefs. God has called us, each with our particular package of gifts, to literally touch the lives of others in His name.

Dick Fenn and I had many occasions to discuss my future either in law or in a church role that would help in the area of law and government. He encouraged me to go to law school or work on a specialized degree to serve in an advocacy role for our church. We prayed often about that and concluded that God would direct in what should happen in that area of my life. For the time being, I would be faithful in my current assignment and go back to college and complete my B.A. degree.

As Eliseo and I reflected on our ministry in Fresno, we thanked God for all the blessings of the growing churches, the advancing Latino youth program, and the successful governmental efforts for our people. He encouraged me never to stop growing. As I reflected on that, I concluded that the day we stop growing, we begin to stagnate and stop leading. I was ready to go back to school and finish my degree.

I called Pastor Benavides. When he heard me say that I intended to go back to school, he congratulated me on the decision and counseled me to "stay close to the Lord." In a reflective tone, he spoke as he had years earlier when I was a high school student. "You cannot imagine what God has planned for you. Stay humble and stay on your knees."

CHAPTER SIX

VISIONARIES AND REVOLUTIONARIES?

The time was right. I took seriously the need to go back to college and finish my studies. Eliseo and Jim had joined the chorus initiated by Richard Hamilton. They universally advised a quick return to school. Things moved even quicker when they obtained the support of Charles Cook, our conference president. My challenge was that I had no scholarships and would have to come up with some creative financial arrangements. Pastor Cook put a deal in writing. If I would complete my degree in one year, the conference would sponsor me for the graduate program at Loma Linda. I saw the light and looked forward to going back to school.

Ruthie and I left Fresno and settled among the palm trees in Loma Linda just across the street from the medical center. She obtained a surgical technician job at Loma Linda, having worked in a similar capacity the previous six years at Saint Helena and Fresno community hospitals. The hospital immediately appreciated her technical skills.

Niels-Erik Andreasen—"I'll be there with you."

I went to La Sierra and met with Dr. Niels-Erik Andreasen, then the associate dean of the school of religion. We worked out a great plan for me to repeat certain classes from my coursework at PUC and structured the last of the requirements in

89

order to finish the work in one year. My degree would be in religion, and I knew before I started that it would not be an easy school year.

Some courses I would take by exam; others would be joined in quarters that would cover as many as 27 units. There was no room for vacillation. Either I did the work or not. Dr. Andreasen saw to it that I didn't lose sight of just how critical it would be that I kept my grades up. For the rest of my program at La Sierra, he personally worked with me to assure me that I could accomplish every goal. He once said to me, "Don't worry; I'll be there with you." And he kept his promise.

Charles and Marta Teel—"Visionaries and revolutionaries"

I enjoyed going back to school because I now was attending out of a desire to be there. I had specific ideas of what I wanted to do in ministry. Consequently, college held promise for me and I could foresee the benefits in my mind. Also the other students on campus considered me old at 26, which gave me the opportunity to be a mentor to others.

The coursework took on a new flavor for me. By the time I sat in those classrooms I had been involved in direct ministry for almost eight years. As with my PUC experience in which I had the Windsor church to work with during my studies, something similar happened at La Sierra. While I was there, an emergency occurred at the San Bernardino Spanish church. The pastor had to leave suddenly to help another church. The Southeastern California Conference asked me to pastor it for a stipend. My wife and I prayed, knowing that we could use the small added income, and we accepted.

It also signaled another transition for me. I had by then benefited from wonderful mentors whom the Lord had sent me to lay key foundational concepts of leadership in my life. Now I would encounter some specific building blocks to place on that foundation. The focus that I received at La Sierra would trigger a series of rapid developments that I could never have anticipated.

Each professor became a friend and colleague during my studies. One that stood out immediately was Dr. Charles Teel, one of the "Wise Men from the East," (he had done his doctoral work at Harvard University). I found myself quickly absorbed by his brilliance and authenticity. Those who know Charles Teel understand that "what you see is what you get." The man can quickly, and sometimes loudly, impress upon you the point he is making.

But that is precisely the beauty of Charles Teel. He holds to a wonderful list of convictions about life, about community, and about our absolute obligation to do something to affect both. His wife, Marta, is also a wonderful leader both in ideas and in how to mobilize people and institutions. Also "of the Harvard ilk," she delightfully enhances the work the couple has developed faithfully for many years.

It is as if they must never sleep! The Teels continuously stir people into action. Studying the lives of Fernando and Ana Stahl, Adventist missionaries to Peru during the early part of the twentieth century, Charles Teel brought out the decisive role of social action in mission. Teel's work has also shown that others, including Yale University and the government of Peru, have also documented that the Adventist missionary work of the Stahls directly changed the fabric of the entire Peruvian nation. The story of the Stahls reflects that of other famed Adventist missionaries. Our difficulty in recognizing that fact has stemmed from the way we have perceived what our missionaries did. Too often we overlook key elements of what great missionaries do to spread God's work abroad.

The Stahls arrived in a country in which a privileged few oppressed the rest. The great majority of Peru's citizens, especially the indiginous people who lived on the Altiplano, were illiterate and powerless to contribute to or lead their own nation. Injustice was commonplace and often the doing of the government itself.

In a paper that refers to the Stahls as "visionaries and revolutionaries" Teel shows convincingly that what the Stahls did was complicated only because of its very simplicity. They set out to establish schools in the Altiplano, particularly focusing on the area of Lake Titicaca. As the system of schools became a part of the lives of the poor, the institutions began to expand and grow in number.

With education came knowledge, dignity, and self-respect among the poor. A natural result of such growth was a desire to shape their own world and lead. As the few in power realized that the Stahls were succeeding in planting an Adventism that brought education and empowerment to the people, a violent reaction resulted.

The Stahls faced serious attacks and threats to their lives. Some people died in the violence that followed. In 1997 a special march and ceremonies in the Altiplano honored the memory of the peasants who had been forced to march into captivity. The celebration retraced their steps. The government of Peru officially recognized the event and its president personally planned to be there. But because of a national emergency at the time, President Fujimori was unable to attend. Even without his presence the event brought greater goodwill between our denomination and the people of Peru.

What the Stahls accomplished still speaks loudly to us today. Charles Teel stresses that what God did in Peru He can still do through His people all around the globe! The themes of the Stahl's ministry became mine also. I now purposed in my heart that I wanted to "go and do likewise."

Charles knew when to carry me and when to watch me flutter awkwardly. He taught me to fly higher than I had ever soared in my previous experience in ministry. If I was to reach new heights in changing my world, I would need greater focus and discipline. Teel pushed me, and sometimes pushed very hard. I learned that to make the transition from belief in the cause of justice to focused action for that cause requires a strong, long-term flying ability. All of this drove me to depend upon the Lord as never before. God consistently renewed my strength and I learned to "mount up with wings like an eagle." God must have smiled as my wings grew stronger every day.

Each quarter at La Sierra took me further than I had planned for. No longer merely fulfilling the minimum requirements for my classes, now I did as much as I could to learn. As the school year came to an end, I had completed my required course work and was ready for graduation! My professors celebrated with me as I prepared to enter my graduate studies in Griggs Hall at Loma Linda.

On graduation day I marched with the brightly colored cords around my neck indicating that I had made decent grades. For the very first time in my entire life, I had good grades! My parents and family were there to celebrate with me. David Taylor had been right—I did have a brain after all. And as he had insisted years earlier, I had learned to use it. Following the graduation ceremony, Prof. Andreasen walked up and hugged me. In his distinctive soft voice he said, "I knew you could do it. I'm proud of you."

Paul Landa—"Only perfect work gets an 'A'."

The Central California Conference followed through with their commitment to sponsor me in my graduate studies. Ruthie and I celebrated when we received my first stipend check. We were especially glad that we would have no more tuition bills since my employer was covering them.

During our time in Loma Linda a young couple became like family to us. David and Sonia Lopez had been friends since our days at Pacific Union College. We all dated our spouses at about the same time and had reconnected in Loma Linda. When Ruthie and I faced any painful situation at the university, Dave and Sony were consistently there. As I progressed in my education, talks with David would help to see me through the occasional discouragements. Sony also become close to Ruthie as our lives blossomed into the eventual births of our children.

I enrolled at Griggs Hall in Loma Linda and soon launched into a master's degree program in religion. My emphasis would be more sociological, so I picked courses that would best help me reach my objectives. There were, however, a few courses required of everyone, regardless of the programs.

One was Introduction to Research Methods. Dr. Paul Landa taught it, and students knew that the ride would not be easy. He had a reputation for his clear and difficult standards and was truly a brilliant scholar. On the first day of class Landa announced, "Only perfect work gets an A." Some laughed out loud because they thought he was joking.

The laughter quickly stopped as he told us that the purpose of the course was to teach us how to do professional-level research that would produce publishable work. Dr. Landa made it abundantly clear that when we left his course at the end of the quarter, we would have either succeeded or failed in our scholarly goals. He reasoned that if we were truly doing graduate work with the potential for postgraduate doctoral studies, we needed these skills. If someone could not accomplish it, he stated, that individual should consider other pursuits.

The course challenged me more than any other class in my life. I had celebrated the idea of a good working brain at my college graduation, but had not counted on needing brilliance too. I could not even perceive myself the kind of advanced scholar Landa expected to produce. When I called Dr. Taylor, he advised me to "pray, hunker down, and study like crazy." Then he added further, "Remember, you've already proven that you have the discipline, now refine it. Don't panic. God is with you."

Throughout my year in the master's program I was able to do the work required of me. Over time I discovered that the studies were actually fun. One day I even entertained the idea that I should remain in the southern California area and do doctoral studies also. My conference administrators quickly put an end to that thought.

That following Christmas Eve, at 10:45 p.m., our first daughter, Veronica, was born. The Lord had smiled on us and given us a wonderful little girl as a Christmas gift. Veronica attended most of the course requirements for a master's degree, although I don't think they would have given her the diploma. My daughter lay quietly in her carrier for up to four hours in some classes and took her bottle or diaper changes without crying once. She reminded me of her mother: gentle, patient, and loving.

Becoming a father during my graduate studies did not hinder my work in any way. Little Veronica actually gave me more reason for living as well as the promise of a joyful future. I was still reading as many as five books a week with corresponding response papers for my different courses each quarter. Also I would work methodically on assignments and then dedicate time to the dreaded final paper for Dr. Landa.

What made it so demanding was the need for perfection. The paper could not exceed 12 pages, and the argument needed to be simple and flawless, with a thesis statement and supporting evidence. Landa expected us to use perfect footnotes, meaning that not a single comma or period or spacing could be out of place. He wanted the grammatical structure in each sentence to be the best possible expression for that idea. For example, he might mark you down if you said something like "It was no small task." You had to say instead, "We worked very hard!"

When we challenged Dr. Landa on this after the midterm, he calmly said, "If you publish a paper in a professional journal, you must say what you mean and mean what you say." He pointed out that too often a scholar is misunderstood because of verbose and confusing scholarly jargon. Landa explained that his job was to teach us to put out a coherent paper containing deep thoughts in simple, concise words. I could not help thinking to myself, *That's just what Jesus did: deep thoughts in simple, concise words.*

My worst fears about the last day of Dr. Landa's class came true, however. One day after we had turned in our assigned papers and accompanying evidence of research, he handed back the graded documents. We heard various moans as people looked at their scores. Some students, who had never had anything lower than an A in their lives, stared at a big bright C or D on their paper. One student talked of suing Dr. Landa, but he countered by saying that we had had an entire quarter to prepare our research. I had to admit that he was right.

During each class session throughout the quarter he had taken us through the techniques of research. We could bring our actual note cards and primary sources, ask any technical question, and even turn in drafts of our paper for his comments and suggestions. Many did not do this and ended up paying the price. Although every aspect of the course was new and painful for me, I could not help concluding that Dr Landa had also been fair.

I received a B and he declared it one of the two "highest scoring papers." No one got an A. Dr. Landa publicly stated that I should consider going into doctoral studies. Having always been the "failing student" while growing up, I could hardly adjust to the idea of now being a "good student."

Another issue that I could not resolve at the time was the value of the course for me. How would any of it be important to my future? What would I do with this information in my ministry? How would the course benefit my career? The Lord would reveal the answers to my questions in a short time.

The end of the school year came, and once again I was ready for graduation. The ceremony convened at the University church in Loma Linda with a capacity crowd attending. Once again I wore bright-colored cords around my neck and praised God when I marched up to the platform to receive my second degree in two years. Many things went through my mind. I had come to get a degree, and ended up receiving an education. God had blessed my mind.

As he did the year before, Dr. Andreasen again walked up to me and gave me another hug. "This is what it means to achieve," he said. "Now go and translate your achievement into a blessing for the world." I thanked him, and the next week I walked off the campus and back into the world—in the name of Christ.

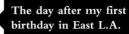

The day after my first birthday in East L.A.

Entering kindergarten, age 5. I had to learn English in a hurry.

The happiest day of my childhood—my ninth birthday party.

December 1970: The day of my dad's baptism.

June 1979: After celebrating the opening of my new church in Windsor, California. I was 19.

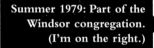

Summer 1979: Part of the Windsor congregation. (I'm on the right.)

My parents, Luis and Stella Rojas—the brave couple whom the Lord blessed.

May 1975: My very first guitar, purchased for $9 at Thrifty's.

My hero, and the pride and joy of my life—my brother Gerry.

October 1976: Leading song service for an outdoor student meeting with John Vigil and Bart Vogel at Monterey Bay Academy.

September 7, 1980: When the woman of my dreams became the woman of my life, Ruth Perez became Ruth Rojas.

The major secret of Ruthie's and my success in ministry has been our prayerful team effort. She sings all the notes that I don't!

My first senior pastor and my best friend, Eliseo Orozco. Serving with him in Fresno was a turning point in my life.

August 1988: Graduation day at Loma Linda University. It's so wonderful to have a brain!

November 1990: Dr. David Taylor dedicates our daughter, Angelica.

January 1994: I will always hang out with young people. This is my calling.

December 1992: With Dr. David Taylor at Gabriel's dedication. My wife, Ruthie, and the girls celebrate.

Pastor Benavides and his wife, Hope. With his computer mind he taught me much about the art of administration.

September 1998: A brief after-dinner discussion regarding various domestic policy issues for which our denomination is recognized as an exemplary leadership entity.

My family today. A very loving and patient group who shares me with many.

November 1992: With their new-born brother, Gabriel, Veronica and Angelica held their dolls with mommy at the hospital.

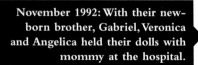

January 1995: Looking for the homeless in St. Louis.

June 1996: I had the joy of carrying the Olympic Torch into Washington, D.C., as the flame made its journey to Atlanta for the Olympic Games.

June 1996: With Maryland's governor Parris Glendening after receiving the Governor's Citation in a ceremony in Annapolis, the state capital.

July 1997: Some of the team I've had the privilege of working with at the North American Division.

January 1997: Ron Whitehead (seated) and Alan Williamson, two pivotal leaders who help make North American youth ministries leadership a success.

The president thanks the Seventh-day Adventist Church for its decisive humanitarian leadership in the country.

CHAPTER SEVEN

"WE'VE GOT TO PRAY YOU THROUGH THIS"

When we returned to the Central California Conference, it assigned me to the Hanford and Goshen Spanish churches just south of Fresno. The area is a lush agricultural region. Although we had heard of the extensive dairy operations in the valley, we had never lived near a dairy before, and we discovered that many of them surround Hanford. Cows have their own way of letting you know their presence. But we also found that you can quickly adjust to new sights, sounds—and odors.

We were excited to discover that while we had been in school Dr. Taylor had been elected the conference executive secretary. The man who had supervised my ministerial training at PUC would now oversee my ministerial work in Central California! He who had performed our wedding and encouraged me while studying in La Sierra would now be only 30 miles away from my church district.

Each of the two churches in my new district had its own special uniqueness. The Hanford Spanish church has a historical significance in our denomination because it is the church building mentioned in *Review and Herald* articles as one of the places Ellen White preached during her visits to central California. The pulpit in the church is "her pulpit" and is still preserved in its original luster. The Goshen church was located just outside of Visalia next to Highway 99 in a small hamlet of older established homes.

The people of the district represent a wide variety of professions and bring great gifts to brighten the congregations. While we served there we even had the mayor of Hanford, Art Brieno, serving as our first elder! Ruthie and I both felt excited by the new challenge and, with lots of prayer, jumped into it with gusto.

But our experience in the Hanford/Goshen district was short-lived. We did not stay there long. After only eight months the conference said that they needed us in Bakersfield at the southernmost end of the valley. The district also included the Lamont Spanish church. Dr. Taylor contacted us to discuss the need and to answer our questions. Our new conference president, Herb Broekel, also strongly encouraged us to take the Bakersfield and Lamont churches. After praying about it, we accepted the call.

When we arrived in Bakersfield we were greeted by a bilingual ministry in which one congregation of about 320 members successfully ministered in two languages. The studies I had just completed at La Sierra and Loma Linda had especially prepared me for the assignment. My graduate work had centered on the use of English among Latinos in the United States. Ruthie and I realized that God had connected us with a prime location to further develop the new cross-cultural potential of Latino ministry.

The Lamont congregation, with about 100 members, was located in an agricultural area east of the city. The members of the church were very active in ministry and made us feel part of the family immediately upon our arrival. Both churches were eager for a master plan in ministry. They wanted to adopt more intentional planning and structured budgeting.

Unlike my previous experiences in ministry, I now perceived my role in more professional and deliberate ways. This time I began by working closely with the elders and the board to develop a shared vision, complete with documented strategic plans. I called Pastor Benavides and told him that I wanted his counsel as I entered a planning phase with my churches. I had committed myself to developing strategic and implementation documents with three to five year grids. Also I wanted to establish realistic budgets that anticipated the developmental growth we projected. For Pastor Benavides this was the equivalent of telling him I was moving from singing in a folk trio to conducting the London Philharmonic Orchestra.

Benavides possesses some of his greatest gifts in the area of administration. Leadership and the intricacies of structure are part of his very being. He can think so scientifically that his analysis and strategic thinking become important tactical tools in an organization. It did not surprise me to learn that he had served on several General Conference committees.

With his valuable mentoring support I moved quickly with my church boards. The resulting initiatives were invigorating. We arranged with three other Adventist churches in the city to support a weekly meals program for the homeless. Also we implemented a plan to train lay members in teaching, public speaking, and evangelism. Within the first year we saw 25 of our own members qualify for the lay preacher credential issued by the conference. In addition, each year we conducted two evangelistic crusades, one for each church. The Lord blessed us, and we saw an average of 60 people baptized each year.

We grew to the point that we needed more ministerial help. When the conference informed us that it had no budget for another minister, we prayed together as churches and asked God to lead us in what we should do. With the conference's blessing we raised money and brought in two assistant pastors to help with the growing work. After a search process, the Lord sent us Pastor Agustin Andrade and his wife, Carmen, whom we assigned to work in the Lamont church, and Saul Castillo and his wife, Rosie, who came to work in Bakersfield.

As Eliseo Orozco had done with me, I made it a point to spend time with both assistant pastors. We visited together often and frequently analyzed each visit in the car. At times we didn't know what to do with a tough situation and would pray together until God showed us. The moments were precious. Both young pastors brought great blessings to the district and the work in both churches continued to flourish.

In the South Valley the Adventist pastors of the 14 churches in the Bakersfield area worked closely through a ministerial association. We had monthly meetings to focus our evangelistic vision and set goals to coordinate more harmonious cross-cultural ministry. There I met pastors who would become wonderful friends for life. A special sense of community exists among the Bakersfield area ministries, a coalition that includes the San Joaquin Adventist Hospital and the Pacific Health Education Center.

One of the pastors I met was Joe Mallinson. As the associate pastor of the Bakersfield Central church, he worked with the senior pastor, Dave Bostrom, in a highly aggressive program of evangelism. As I look back at my experiences in Bakersfield, these men come to mind as part of the joy of "team soul winning" that occurred among our churches. We worked together on the meals project that grew to serve more than 500 homeless people each week. In addition, we produced coordinated crusades that brought a joint evangelistic vision with the other churches and a triumphant baptism at a lake just outside of town.

One day the conference youth director, John Loor, Jr., phoned me and asked for an appointment. Later he came down to Bakersfield and met me for lunch. John spoke of a plan that the conference had under way to assign a "youth pastor" in each of eight areas of the conference to oversee the youth programming. He needed help in carrying out the growing demands of the youth department. Our conference had about 8,000 youth, and John was setting up a team of specialists to stay ahead of the need.

I asked him for time to pray with Ruthie about the offer, especially since the assignment would be in addition to my current pastoral duties with my two churches. When I talked with Ruthie, she was very enthusiastic about the potential of reaching the youth in the South Valley. Then I called Joe Mallinson to ask his counsel, and he agreed with Ruthie that it would be good for us and for our youth. He even offered to help me with the tasks. Joe then prayed with me over the phone.

The next day I called John to inform him that I accepted the responsibility. Thanking me, he then asked if I would mind also assuming the conference Mexico Mission trip that took place once a year. I realized that it translated into an enormous amount of work, but I also knew that John had carried the full load of senior youth, camping, and Pathfinders for several years and critically needed the help. Giving in, I agreed to add the mission trip to the assignment.

Pastor Frank Valdez—"Remember to think of a name . . ."

As time progressed in Bakersfield, the Lord blessed our labors. I marveled at how He had brought us this far, although we paid difficult prices. Fatigue frequently dogged us, but the Lord always sustained us. I now had to learn how to control the quantity of work that I allowed myself. It became very easy to overwork.

Another sign that pointed to our need to slow down was in the difficulty Ruthie had when she became pregnant again. We had no idea what a miscarriage was like, but we found out that it can be extremely devastating, causing real grief in the life of a couple. After three traumatic miscarriages, we wondered if we would ever have another child. Not knowing what to do, I called Dr. Taylor.

After a fatherly discussion, we decided to take the matter formally to the Lord in prayer. Ruthie and I invited Dr. David Taylor and Pastor Frank Valdez, another friend from my L.A. days, to our home the next week. That night the two men arrived with a vial of oil. After reading from the Word of the Lord we knelt around Ruthie as hands were laid on her in prayer. Both Dr. Taylor and Pastor Valdez anointed her gently with the oil, asking God to intervene and give us a child according to His will.

Ruthie and I authentically experienced the presence of the Lord that night as we prayed. We had no particular emotional feeling, and I can't say that anything magical happened. All we know is that we became absolutely certain that God was in charge and that He had a plan. Before leaving, Frank said, "Remember to think of a name for your baby." Our grief turned into peace as we waited upon the Lord.

A few weeks later Ruthie was not feeling well. When we confirmed that she was pregnant, we went back to God on our knees. There we affirmed our trust in the Lord and His ability to provide for our family. Ruthie had to rest a lot and changed her regular schedule. The doctors were optimistic. After the first trimester we knew that God had done a wonderful work.

Some months later our daughter Angelica was almost born in the car as we rushed to the hospital! When the Lord answers prayer, things almost go too well! Our other daughter Veronica immediately began bonding with her little sister as our two churches lovingly surrounded us like an extended family. David Taylor traveled down to Bakersfield on a Wednesday night to dedicate Angelica. As he literally held our daughter up in the air before the Lord, Ruthie and I huddled close to dedicate to God the child He had given us so graciously.

Not long after that the ministerial association elected me its chairman while we were away on vacation! When I returned and learned that a meeting was coming up and that I had to prepare the materials, I was touched that my colleagues in town trusted me and wanted me to be a part of their joint vision of leadership. I accepted the role, and we set out to plan the yearly convocation that brings together all the churches at the convention center in Bakersfield. All seemed good and marching according to plan, but a massive shadow loomed in the horizon. I could have never prepared for what was to come next.

Joseph Mallinson—"We've got to pray you through this."

We drove down to Los Angeles just over the mountain from our house about 120 miles away. The palm trees stood quietly, almost as if they were watching us as we drove through town. When we arrived at my aunt's house, my brother Gerry's wife and my aunt were visiting together in her living room. Seeing us, both women suddenly broke into tears. I quickly said that I had come because I had not heard from Gerry in a while. When I asked them to tell me where he was they had to leave the room. The two women huddled in the kitchen and cried loudly.

Following them, I insisted that they tell me where Gerry was. My aunt turned to me and, with great hesitation, said, "I'm afraid he is no longer with us." Attempting to absorb what she was saying, I asked quietly, "You mean he's dead?" At that, both women again cried loudly as my aunt confirmed with a trembling nod the worst news I had ever heard.

I walked them back to the living room and collected myself with two deep breaths. For the next 45 minutes I calmly asked all the questions I could about my brother's death. "Where is he?" I asked. "I want to see his body." My aunt answered that he had been dead for more than four months. Suddenly I felt faint. My immediate family had two ordained ministers, and we didn't get to bury our own brother.

"How did he die?" My aunt could say only that no one knew for sure. "What are the police saying?" I continued.

"They closed the case in less than three days!"

"Where did he die?"

"On Hancock Street, near the corner of Mission and Main."

"Why did he die?"

"We don't know."

"Who killed him?"

"We don't know."

"Were there any witnesses?"

"Yes; several people saw it happen."

Then I asked the most difficult question: "Why didn't you tell us months ago?" Both women trembled and held each other as they tried to explain why they had said nothing to our mother and we, his brothers and sister. I realized that there was no real answer. Things had just snowballed out of control when Gerry died. Since the immediate family lived far from the city, no one phoned us, and after a time, nobody wanted to be the one to come late with the news. Consequently, time just passed, and we never learned about it until I happened to drop by unannounced.

I felt totally numb. As we drove through the city on our way home, Ruthie clung to me without saying anything, allowing me to absorb the enormity of the blow. The beautiful palm trees that distinguish Los Angeles now seemed like cold, indifferent witnesses to our tragedy. The light haze of pollution that looms over the skyline reminded me of just how polluted and lonely our world of sin really is. As we drove along the Golden State Freeway, I looked at many smiling people who didn't know, or care, that my brother was gone. Finally, on the mountain along Highway 5, as we were leaving the town of Valencia, I suddenly had a great need to pull off the freeway.

When I stopped at a McDonald's restaurant, my emotions finally caught up with me, and I experienced the deepest and most indescribable pain I have ever known. My Gerry, my hero and the hope of my childhood, was gone. He was already buried someplace that I hadn't even been to. I had seen him last on his birthday and had taken him out to eat. His final words to me the next morning during our last embrace were "I love you, Joe." Now I was devastated, lost without the security of his presence.

The drive to Bakersfield was a blur, a bizarre dream. I kept wondering if I would wake up and realize that it all was just a horrific nightmare that would wear off during breakfast. But that was not to be. Back in Bakersfield, I went about the difficult task of calling my siblings. I phoned Louie. He was pastoring a church in Albuquerque, New Mexico, and I knew that two preachers could at least discuss this without losing all control. Louie had also been a chaplain in his career and possessed wonderful skills in listening and grief recovery. I trusted him to help me as well as to suggest ideas for "how to tell Mom."

As expected, Louie was a tower of stability and strength when talking with me, and he immediately agreed to call our sister Martha in Tacoma, Washington, to inform her. We further agreed that he and Martha would come to Bakersfield the next day so that we could drive up to Ukiah and tell Mom together. It was not something that we could announce over the phone. Our other brother, Ruben, lived in a building on my parents' property, and we would have to notify him only moments before we would see Mom.

The next day Louie and Martha arrived at our home, and we set off on our long drive of about seven hours to northern California. When we reached Ukiah and got out of the car, it was an unusually dark night, and a cold rain was falling. Our souls were also dark, cold, and dampened by the tears of loss. We walked into Ruben's room and awoke him. Because we all live so far away, he knew that something was wrong. We told him the news as he threw on some clothes and we prepared to see Mom inside the house.

Dad was there too. We were afraid how he would react. Since Gerry was my mother's son by a previous marriage, and Dad and he had never gotten along, we knew that guilt might overwhelm him. Gerry's childhood had been terrible, and unpleasant memories might further complicate Mom's grief.

As we entered the house my mother saw me first. She quickly lit up with a smile and asked why I hadn't let her know that I was coming over. Then she saw Martha, Louie, finally Ruben. Mom grew quiet and took a deep breath. One of the great truths of life is that a mother can usually read her children at first glance. With a breaking voice my mother said, "Something has happened. Why are you all here?"

As her eyes began to gloss over, we all knelt around her, and my mom braced for the worst. Gently, and with the softest euphemisms we could produce, we broke the news that no parent ever wants to receive. My mother had watched her mom die when she was a child and had sat next to her dad when he died in a car wreck the next year. She had survived real pain and therefore was no stranger to trauma. Our instinct about being together at that moment proved to be the best thing we could have done for her.

As my mother wept, she held us close. As a chicken gathers her chicks, she pulled her grown children near, smoothing our hair and touching us. She thanked God that her remaining children were with her at that terrible moment. Amazingly, it was my mom who comforted us. She who had every reason to be destroyed kept us from falling apart. Once again I marveled at her strength.

The following day we all drove down to Los Angeles and went to the cemetery where Gerry had been buried. There Louie, Martha, and I conducted a memorial service. As we stood over a mound of dirt that some piece of paper claimed now contained my brother's body, once again nature paralleled our souls. The cold February Santa Ana winds blew relentlessly, causing us to tremble and bow in our thick coats. We had to shout awkwardly to be heard over the roar in our ears. I didn't get to touch a casket or have the privilege of saying goodbye to him. At that cold moment I wondered if I would ever heal.

When I returned to Bakersfield, the first thing I did was to resign from my youth ministry assignments with John Loor. Also I felt completely unable to carry out my duties with the ministerial association. Soon I slipped into a pattern of anger. For several weeks I could not attend my churches. Instead I went to Los Angeles and conducted my own investigation of Gerry's death. Visiting the Los Angeles County Morgue, I bought a copy of Gerry's autopsy report. There I discovered the cause of his death. Then I went to police headquarters in downtown Los Angeles and obtained a copy of the police report.

I did not like what I was uncovering, however. Gerry had died as a result of homicide, but his death certificate officially listed "accidental death." Many irregularities had occurred, because, as the police detective told me, he died in "the wrong part of town." His body was in terrible condition when someone finally called the police to report his death. The police investigator who handled his case explained that they have so many deaths in East Los Angeles that they have to close cases as soon as they can. Although several witnesses had been there, the authorities did not seriously follow up, because that would complicate the case. The two men who killed Gerry walked away free.

After my personal investigation I failed to notice that I had stopped praying. Prayer had become my most vital connection with the Lord. When prayer falters, everything begins to fall apart. I was not aware that I had moved from having grief to an uncontrollable grief having me. Such things are very subtle. They can creep up on you when you're not looking. One afternoon I finally got into my car and angrily decided to drive up to the conference office in Fresno and turn in my credentials. I was going to resign from the ministry.

When I reached the Selma exit along Highway 99, just 15 miles short of the exit to the conference office, I pulled off the freeway. What I was about to do suddenly and deeply struck me, and I remember crying uncontrollably over my steering wheel. I had hit bottom. I could not feel any lower than I did at that moment. Frantically I looked around at the cars driving by, but no one noticed my need. Selma is the very town in which I had preached my first sermon when I was 16 years old. It was as if I had made a full circle and had returned to the place where it all began, to ponder an end to ministry. Nothing seemed to matter at that desperate and dark moment. There was nowhere to look—but up.

In that moment of deepest need, when we have no choice but to face what hurts us the most, then it is that God can reach out to us. With my head over the steering wheel, I prayed. I cried out to the Lord, asking why He had allowed this to happen. There was no answer. Suddenly it filled me with horror to think that I had almost reached the conference office to resign from the ministry! As I shook my head, I regained composure and reentered the freeway to drive the 70 miles south back to Bakersfield.

Ruthie was worried yet very understanding and patient with me through this time. When she saw me that evening, she advised me to call someone I trusted. I immediately phoned Joe Mallinson and asked to see him. He quickly met me in his church. I cried as I spilled my heart to him, sharing my frustration that the pastors I had already approached did not know how to help me. It seems that loss from homicide is different than from that of accidents or illnesses. It also frustrated me that I knew the biblical passages pertaining to death and thus did not respond as someone else who needs to hear them.

Joe reached across and placed his hand on my shoulder.

"We have to pray you through this," he said, adding, "You don't need a sermon, and you don't need the 'right words,' either." As I looked up at him, he almost whispered, "You need healing, José. You need to know God is near." We knelt together, and Joe prayed. God reached across that night and touched my broken heart.

Late that night I called Dr. Taylor and awoke him out of his sleep. I knew that he understood the pain of the mean streets. He explained to me how he had lost friends and relatives under similar circumstances. As with Joe earlier in the evening, I once again knew that God was near. "Let's pray," Taylor said. During his prayer it became very clear to me that God had been there all along. He had never turned His back on me. Indeed, I was the one who turned away whenever I didn't see Him.

I am constantly amazed at how patient and loving God is in such circumstances. We begin our grief by wondering how a God of love can allow something like this to happen. Then we move to blaming Him for the evil in this world. Imagine—we blame God for what the devil does to us! But God Himself knows what it is to grieve because He too lost His only Son to the curse of death on this planet.

But just as He lost His Son to death, He came to see Him again in the resurrection. The same God who grieves with us when we lose a loved one will be coming soon to put an end to life's unfairness. God did not invent evil, but He will finish with it soon. For the first time I began to look toward the coming of Jesus with a new expectation. The words of the apostle took on new meaning as I reached a personal understanding of what he meant by "the blessed hope" of Christ's return.

But the greatest miracle in my ministry was about to come. Through this terrible experience of losing my oldest brother, as I found new strength, God poured out a powerful blessing. I had always heard people testify that God can turn trauma into blessing. I know that he did this for Leslie Goodwin throughout his life. But I finally understood personally just how true it is.

I am a preacher. Ever since Kenny Utecht introduced me to public ministry, my experiences had increased. By this time in my life I was known as a "good preacher." I even often traveled across the country and around the world to speak for all kinds of ministry events for both youth and adults. But this was different. I cannot quite explain it in words. As I resumed preaching for the Lord, a new Spirit attended me when I spoke. It is the only way I know how to describe it.

Ruthie and I noticed it immediately. Although I preached with the same methods, without notes, from memory, as I had already done for several years, the impact was overwhelmingly different. God began to take my sermons and turn them into miraculous encounters with the Holy Ghost. One day as I preached I was brought almost to tears as it dawned on me that *I too* was learning something from what I had just said during my sermon!

With Gerry's passing I felt that there was no more that I could lose. I gave myself completely to the Lord when I preached and now spoke with an unmistakable passion. I became so absorbed in my sermons that I even began to act out the scenes in my narrative style of presentation. My preaching ministry increased so dramatically that Ruthie and I asked God, "Why do we need this kind of preaching?"

What we were experiencing was not normal and certainly not natural. I have never publicly confessed this part of my testimony because it is difficult to explain. I consulted with Pastor Benavides and Eliseo Orozco individually. We were all mystified by the development and decided that the Lord knew what He was doing. They each prayed with me, perhaps not realizing the deep trouble I was feeling over the new impact of my preaching. The stress over my preaching increased as I suddenly began to receive large numbers of invitations from around the world.

The elders of my church sat me down one day to discuss my "new problem" of increased travel away from my district. I became very afraid. What was God doing? Why was the Lord attending my preaching in this way? The extraordinary growth in my responsibility of "rightly dividing the word of truth" was a stressful transition in my life. Shifting from what appears to be merely a "good sermon" to a "powerful sermon" brings untold pressures to have to cope with.

A person can easily fall into the temptation of thinking that successful preaching results from personal gifts and talents. But Ruthie and I clearly recognized that suddenly, one day, God had made this transition happen. I still felt the same as I had always felt before, with all my planning for a sermon and my style of delivery. But once I got to a platform and began to speak, we could sense the movement of the Holy Spirit in astonishing ways. A preacher must plan the outline for the material. The topic needs to be fitted to the needs of the listeners. But when a minister ascends to the platform to preach of the kingdom of heaven, only the Lord can be trusted to communicate effectively that message. God uses the preacher to accomplish that task.

With the process of healing at work in my life, I again resumed my assignments with youth ministries and the ministerial association. Pastor Robert Folkenberg, our denomination's world president, accepted our invitation to attend the convocation at the convention center. We chose the Global Mission theme as our objective for finishing God's work in the South Valley. The meetings went well, and our people felt inspired to work harder for the Lord. I purposed in my heart to labor harder for the Lord as well.

CHAPTER EIGHT

"GO GET 'EM, LITTLE BUDDY"

Not long after that convocation in Bakersfield I received a phone call from our conference president, Herb Broekel. He told me that he wanted me to come to Fresno soon and lead senior youth ministries. There was a move under way to separate senior youth from the camping and Pathfinder programs so that two people could once again carry the ministry as had been done in years past. I really didn't think that would happen any time soon, so I didn't give it another thought.

The next week. however, Herb called back to tell me that the other departmental directors had voted to recommend my name to the personnel committee for the position. Now I stopped to think about what was happening. I remembered how, years earlier, I had told our previous youth director, Richard Hamilton, that I wanted to prepare for youth ministry. He had challenged me to "be like Christ" when I worked with youth. I found his counsel to be true. As long as I sought to be Christ-like with youth, the ministry had grown.

Soon afterward Herb phoned yet again to officially invite me to serve as the senior youth and family ministries director for Central California Conference. He mentioned that the vote on the executive committee had been unanimous. Overwhelmed, I asked for two days to pray with Ruthie and seek the Lord's guidance. We struggled because we were so deeply committed to Bakersfield and Lamont. Our church members were hoping we would not leave.

Two days later we were certain that the Lord had directed the call, and we accepted. We were moved that our church members agreed with the decision. One couple, Jesse Jordan and his wife, Marie, had been counseling us about the offer. Jesse told us that the time had come to enter church leadership and that we needed to advance with courage.

Our farewell at our churches was very difficult. We had bonded so deeply that everything now just came too suddenly. We felt honored that our relationship was as good as it was in our congregations. Packing our things again, we headed back north to Fresno.

By the time we went to work at the conference office, David Taylor had accepted the position of vice president in the Pacific Union conference. He left just before I arrived. I felt a sense of loss that I would not get to serve in the same building with him. But I understood how God leads and quickly adjusted to the reality.

Arthur Bushnell—"Go get 'em, little buddy!"

Once I arrived at the conference office I met with my immediate superior, Pastor Art Bushnell, and asked him what he expected of me. After reviewing the job description in the official call, he simply concluded that he wanted me to "go out and do what you are known for with kids." I had not been aware that I "was known" in that way. Art said that he expected me to use creativity in developing an agenda with my team for youth leadership. He then prayed with me and asked God to bless my tenure in this new ministry. As we concluded our meeting I asked, "Anything else you want to say to me as I begin?"

"Go get 'em, little buddy!" he replied in his usual deep voice.

For the next year and a half I worked with a wonderful group of people. In the office John Loor became a key confidant and mentor. He believed in me and offered good advice on many issues. In the treasury I could count on Eleanor, Peggy, and Shirley as financial advisors and friends who cared not only about my department's ledger numbers, but also my family.

Another person who became a trusted friend was Bobby

McGhee. As a Bible teacher at Fresno Academy at the time, I can best describe him as an incredibly creative guy who loves Jesus and brings Him into people's lives. Bobby helped in planning events and the occasional crisis when the anniversary of my brother's death would roll by. What I remember most fondly about him was the moments when we prayed together in my office.

During the time I served at the conference office we also saw a bold move in the Bay area in which a youth pastor, David Wood, served for a time in a strong local youth ministry organization. My friend Jim Pimentel had an important part in making that happen. Jim didn't realize it, but I still looked back to the days when *he* encouraged me to "focus and specialize." Not long after that, the conference assigned him to assist me with different aspects of the youth department.

Now that Jim and I were working together again, I pulled out his letter from years earlier in which he had looked to the day when we would work together. Some of my mentors may not always recognize how much they contributed to my life. But that just goes to show that you cannot always fully understand the extent of the impact you can make on another. I have always done my best to emulate Jim's precision and professionalism. He transformed me forever.

As I developed a larger youth ministry program for the Central California Conference, I traveled a lot to many local churches and schools in our territory. There I would preach with a growing conviction and passion. My relationship with youth increased and I knew that my life would reflect new experiences. I attended Weeks of Prayer, Youth Days at churches, and other rallies. In my new role I saw that our denomination had barely tapped the surface of what our youth had to offer. Most adults seemed to realize this but were not sure what to do about it.

Young people are the epitome of raw energy. I found in my ministry that they are not interested in being controlled. Whether they are gang members on the street or part of a Sabbath school class in a church, they resist control and the loss of their individuality. Many of the parents and grandparents that I met around the conference asked an eerily similar question: "What is our church going to do with our youth?"

When I would ask youth themselves behind closed doors

about the question, they tended to answer with a question of their own, "Hasn't the church done enough to us?" What became apparent was that many congregations thought of youth as a resource for the future. Consequently, they did not take young people seriously because they assumed, unconsciously or otherwise, that the youth needed to grow up before they could ever contribute to their congregation. Young people reacted to this demeaning attitude with silent rebellions that varied from church to church.

In some places a church would respond by imposing increased rules on the youth, worsening the problem. Unlike adults who can take difficult issues to the church board, a young person can only vote with his or her feet. Many youth began to disappear from churches. The problem seemed to escalate during the 1980s, and by the turn of the 1990s it was at the point of crisis. I knew that the adults who were overreacting to their youth were not bad people. But we clearly had arrived at a point in history where traditional methods and regulations would not work for a new generation of youth. Adults and youth simply were not communicating with each other. Few could hear what the other said.

I turned to my friends in Florida, Sergio and Chari Torres. I had met them the previous year when Sergio invited me to camp meeting in Orlando. While there I was astounded to see what the ministerial couple was accomplishing with youth. Never in my life had I seen such decisive ministry taking the energy of youth in new directions. Instead of the traditional controlling methods of youth leadership, Sergio and Chari succeeded in *focusing* the energy of youth for ministry.

As the associate youth ministries director for the Florida Conference, Sergio works with a strong team of committed professionals and volunteers in an aggressive youth department that mobilizes thousands of youth each year. When I observed with my own eyes what Miami youth could do in the city's streets and churches, I took courage.

The Torres' concept was quite simple: take all the raw energy of youth and give them a vision. As youth give their lives to Christ, there is literally nothing that they cannot do. There in Miami with Sergio and Chari I found a new building block in my ministry: if a gang of teenagers can take over a community in the name of evil, imagine what a group of committed young people can do in that community in the name of Christ!

Sergio and Chari have succeeded in harnessing young people from the churches of Miami and the local academy in new and life-changing ways. They focus on giving young people authority to do specific tasks in team efforts. To the north of Florida, Bill Crofton and Denise Badger, also of the Florida Conference youth ministries, have unleashed young people into their community as never before.

Sergio and Chari developed a Spanish language magazine for local Latino church youth leaders called *Gente Joven* (Young People). In it they build upon the strength of local youth ministry as the foundation for larger ministry initiatives that will succeed in the city. As they worked with individual congregations, the youth groups blossomed in ways I have not often seen. The approach the Torres used was something we wanted to do in Central California. If we could allow our youth to actually lead according to their gifts, the phenomenon could spread across our conference.

I consulted with Sergio and Chari as I prepared to introduce this model in Central California. Central includes major cities such as San Francisco and sprawling metropolitan areas like the Silicon Valley of computer fame. It also has agricultural cities, towns, and villages. The variety and contrasts were enormous, demanding a youth ministry that can adapt to local needs rather than a single method to be used by all.

The work is difficult because it means that a new youthful culture arises in churches unaccustomed to active young people. It can seem threatening when we see them doing things once unheard of among their age group. But I personally knew what God could do. Since the age of 16 I have seen the Lord lead me in preaching, planting churches, working with political leaders and other nontraditional ministry. Even the military knows that if you really want to win a war, you send out the youth. The average age of the soldier who died on the beaches of Normandy was 18. And the average age of the sailors who today handle the awesome power of an aircraft carrier is 19.

As our youth committee worked on our California plan, we began by focusing on training as a core element for Central's new strategy. Then we moved to develop some pilot sites and possible funding projects for them. We dialogued with several of our schools to link educational objectives with the effort. I kept Herb informed of the progress, feeling satisfied that we were gaining ground for our launch. Later I spent a couple days at Mammoth Mountain with Jim Pimentel as we looked at strategic plans for implementing and funding our plan.

While the work progressed, I felt a need to keep myself immersed in a personal ministry. I could not be content with only my office work and the weekend preaching assignments. Being naturally restless, I wanted to be involved in something that would challenge me to continue to grow spiritually while I matured professionally.

After praying about it, I decided to enlarge my ministry for gang members. Having worked with them since my days in Windsor, I took all the opportunities I could to "hang out" with street kids. It was not as if I had a lot of extra time to spare. But Gerry's death had forced me to examine again what I was doing to make a difference on the street. Part of my grief has been to grapple with the fact that many die anonymously on the street and that few people want to do anything about it, except to demand more police and prisons from their politicians. In fact, it appears that many are more accustomed to condemning people on the street than ministering to them.

When Gerry died, he did not die while helping another. He didn't die for his country on the field of battle. Nor did he even die for a cause. My beloved brother died for absolutely nothing. Gerry was buried without his family present. In his autopsy report they mistakingly identified him under the wrong race. My brother's life shrank to a single digit on the Los Angeles homicide report, and even there they listed him under the wrong column. For all intents and purposes, my brother Gerry never existed.

A conviction grew within me that this is not the way of Jesus. I cannot imagine that heaven wants us to lose the sacredness of humanity so brutally. We who have been made in the image of God Himself cannot possibly afford to think of *anyone* as less than ourselves. Regardless of race, color, economic condition, or any other element that tends to separate us as humans, I purposed never again to allow myself the carelessness of doing only "little things" for the powerless. I decided that I would dedicate time for society's marginalized. I took on a personal obligation to all those society actually allowed to die anonymously without the dignity that is the right of all humans.

The mentoring I received from Charles Teel now went into action. I learned from him not to worry about what people think of me when serving those on the edges of society. My convictions were set. I supplemented my ministry for youth in the conference with personal time for tough kids on the street.

I participated in an intervention program in Fresno that brought parents and their at-risk kids together for counseling and joint celebrations. When it identified a kid as someone likely to slide into a gang lifestyle, the Fresno Unified School District worked to help the family stop the threat by bringing them together. Occasionally the school district brought me in as a speaker for such programs and events.

The larger part of the ministry involved actually finding kids on the street. Obviously it had risk because I spent time with armed and angry kids. Many of the kids were the children of parents from my local churches who would then introduce me to their friends. I began to see kids have victory over drugs and make choices for Christ. At times they gave up drug dealing and helped their friends off the street too.

I don't know for sure when it happened, but one day I offended an influential gang member somewhere in Fresno. The best information we have indicates that someone followed me home. For the next year and nine months my family endured some of the most frightening harassment we've ever experienced. The youths first broke the windows on one of my cars and stole the radio and other contents. I wasn't particularly alarmed, because such vandalism is unfortunately common.

But eventually the incidents escalated. Sometimes I would leave my house to go to work only to find that all of our cars were gone. Police became accustomed to going to our house at all hours of the day and night as the attacks increased. Later we began to hear gunshots fired into our van or into the air in front of the house.

By then I was traveling around the world preaching and participating with other leaders in ministry. One day I called home from Guam to see how Ruthie and the kids were doing. My wife calmly told me that my car was gone and that she didn't know where it was. I remember feeling that sense of desperation that comes when you know you can't do anything about a situation. The police could no longer help me, because I was "not bleeding." They had to deal with so many crimes in the city that they could keep up only if they put first priority on those where blood was flowing.

I called the mayor's office and was told something similar. While we were grateful that no gang had ordered me killed, the organized campaign to drive us out of town was having its effect. Some of my own people in the office began to wonder when I "would swallow my pride" and move out of my "bad neighborhood." They had obviously not visited my home, because I lived in a quiet middle-class neighborhood just as they did. But things had clearly gotten out of control, with gunshots and theft a growing problem.

On another occasion I flew to Massachusetts to help Dr. Taylor with a youth training event and a committee. Recently elected the president of the Atlantic Union, he involved me in leadership opportunities with him there. On the afternoon that I returned from Boston, Ruthie went to pick me up at the airport. The house was alone for only a few minutes, but a group in a van was waiting around the corner when she drove away. In that short period of time they kicked our front door in and robbed us, taking almost anything of monetary value.

As we pulled into our driveway, we could see the front door wide open. I carried my luggage into the house and placed it on the floor of our living room; then the extent of the robbery became very evident. The house looked bare except for the larger furniture. One of our cameras still lay on the front lawn, obviously dropped accidentally as the thieves sped away when we rounded the corner coming home.

Then, as if a knife had penetrated my heart, I noticed that my guitar was gone. The same guitar that my parents had sacrificed to buy for me 15 years earlier when I studied at MBA. I had taken it with me to different continents around the world and used it for only one purpose, the preaching of the Word. Breaking into tears, I sat on the steps of my front porch.

The phone rang; it was David Taylor checking to see that I had gotten home all right. He and his wife, Maxine, listened quietly as I told them tearfully what had happened. I even walked around the house, surveying our losses. The timing of their call could not have been more blessed. After sharing words of care and understanding, they prayed with me on the phone and asked God to protect us.

Ruthie was pregnant, and such extreme stress did not help her. Yet she never complained a single time. My wife became a tower of strength during our trying times in Fresno. She prayed with more conviction and vowed that we would not leave Fresno until the Lord called us away! The police had said that if we moved across town to another neighborhood, the gang would simply follow us to the new house. With Ruthie's support I continued to work hard for the youth both of the conference and the kids on the street.

Our pastor in our local church was none other than Pastor Benavides. The privilege of having him as my own church pastor was a wonderful miracle! He worked closely with us to solve our violent dilemma. One day he brought the elders of the church, and we gathered in our home to dedicate our house to the Lord in a similar fashion as a sick person who receives anointing. The plea went heavenward, asking God to form a special protection around us physically as we sought to serve in the name of Christ.

I was surprised at how differently people reacted to our predicament. Once I attended a meeting at which a missionary related how she had served in Africa the previous year, helping underprivileged children and their families. Then she told how extreme violence had broken out, leading to the deaths of many people. She testified as to how God had delivered her through the help of other Christians. I could see the audience visibly inspired and responding with admiration as the young woman told her testimony. Some in the audience exclaimed softly, "What faith!" Others said, "This is real mission, just as the Bible says. This girl is prepared to die for Christ!"

Then it was my turn. I presented almost the same testimony on how I was working with underprivileged youth and their families in Fresno. As I identified the ministry as a "gang-intervention" ministry, some sat back in their seats, looking confused and crossing their arms. I spoke of the youth who had given up drugs and were now helping their friends meet Jesus.

When I asked for prayers because of the continuing violence outside my front door, several began to shake their heads disapprovingly. I heard someone ask another quietly, "Why does he go directly into danger? Doesn't he know that those people want to live that way?" Others asked their neighbor, "Doesn't he care about his family and their safety?"

I walked out of that meeting feeling extremely lonely. It hurt to realize that so many perceive ministry as something that occurs on other continents. When you carry out the exact same tasks here in North America, someone may actually question your judgment. Why is it that we consider social action as "mission" in lands far away, but not here at home? Experience had showed me that we also live in the midst of a giant mission field. My calling, even if it kills me, is to be faithful and serve unto the end. If I worked in Rwanda, most would understand such commitment, but since I'm serving in North America, I knew that it would take time to plant a new mind-set among many of our people.

Facing opposition builds character. It forces a person to evaluate and affirm the values that drive a ministry. Through our terrible trauma of gunshots, thefts, and graffiti threats, Ruthie and I developed a stronger spiritual walk. We lost our insurance for both the house and the vehicles. The police, the mayor's office, and the rest of the system refused to aid us unless we stopped helping kids on the street. But through this, Jesus gave us a more refined armor to cope with the most overwhelming odds in life. Ruthie once commented, "We can survive anything in life after we leave Fresno!" Her words were prophetic—we would need such strength in the future.

About that time Election Day arrived. Ruthie, who was now nine months pregnant, didn't go to vote, because she was not feeling well. That particular day was uneventful. We had heard no shots during the night, and our cars were still on the driveway in the morning. I cast my vote at the polling place and then went to work at the office. Throughout that day I met with leaders and planned an upcoming youth congress for the conference.

That night I stayed up late to watch the election returns. Various House and Senate seats were on my priority list to watch and note the results. As the night progressed I began to realize that change was in the air. President George Bush was not having a good night, as the numbers pointed to the other candidate. At 1:00 in the morning the media projected Bill

Clinton as the presidential winner.

I shouted down the dark hallway to where Ruthie was lying quietly in the bedroom. "Ruthie, we have a new president. Bill Clinton has been elected." Immediately she went into labor! With a deep moan she said that we had better get to the hospital. Her mother came to stay with Veronica and Angelica as we prepared Ruthie's things for her stay at the hospital. Remembering that our previous child had almost been born in the car, we hurried as fast as we could.

When we reached Fresno Community Hospital, our doctor was, of course, home asleep. She would not get there for a long time because she lived more than 40 miles away. The shift physician on duty was caring for an emergency C-section and thus the nurse and I looked at each other with the realization that she and I were in for "delivery duty" that night.

As the most difficult moment of delivery arrived, the nurse skillfully and gently talked Ruthie through the experience. I obediently did as I was told in assisting each step of our child's birth. When our child was finally born, I held my first son in my arms. The nurse and I suctioned his little mouth and secured his umbilical cord. After gently wiping him down and placing a special cream in his eyes, I wrapped Gabriel in a little blue blanket and put him in my wife's arms.

During that first moment of bonding, as Ruthie and I looked at our newest blessing, the nurse spoke to us. She congratulated us for a fine, healthy child. Then she turned to me and said, "And I loved your sermon when you preached at my church last week." It stunned Ruthie and I to learn that the nurse who had just guided my wife through the delivery was a Seventh-day Adventist!

When we brought little Gabriel home two days later, our daughters marveled at the sight of a "little boy" in the house. We were now five in the Rojas household, and the joy of watching my three little ones brought me a sense of what heaven is going to be like. I also learned that love cannot be explained in words as I now looked at Ruthie with the realization that my love for her still continued to grow. Each time I have witnessed her risk her life to give me a child confirmed to me that God is love. Love is so deep that it can only increase. Because of the profoundness of that growth, love becomes our reason for living, always seeking to blossom into new life.

Not long after we settled back into our home with Gabriel, we were reminded that the world had kept turning outside. I had a cold feeling in my heart as we heard gunshots again, with occasional verbal threats from cars driving by at night. By day we continued our ministry and then lived another life at night. Ruthie began to "work the night shift," sitting at the window until around 2:00 a.m. on many nights. I was not aware what she was doing at first, but soon began to take my own night watches.

Often we had to call police to thwart an attempt against us. One night the youths began to steal our neighbor's cars, hurting us even further as neighbors pointed out that "everything was fine until you folks arrived." On another night the gang pipe-bombed a neighbor's truck and the blame fell in our direction. The pressure from our neighbors was subtle, because they really liked us, but we sensed that most wished that we would move away. One night a police officer explained how, if I had a .38 revolver, I could shoot one of these kids and there would be no judge in the world who would allow us to be prosecuted. The suggestion horrified me. I looked into the officer's eyes and with deep conviction said, "God called me to save kids, not kill them." I had come to understand by that point in my life that my commitment to youth was not a career move, but rather a way of life.

The inevitable ultimately happened. Ruthie and I started praying that God would either resolve the situation or get us a call to another ministry away from Fresno. We were disappointed, because I was about to launch the new plan for youth ministries in the conference and I wanted to see it through. But the escalating harassment now had included people following me when I drove around the city. They even vandalized my car in broad daylight while I preached in local churches.

While we were able to stop many incidents of attempted violence or robbery before they happened, 16 incidents did succeed. In the process we lost more than $18,000 in property and damage for which insurance covered only a small portion, because we lost our coverage early on. Our financial situation was grave as we spent additional emergency money on an electronic security system, special lighting for the yard, six-foot fences, an extended driveway, large gates, a 200-pound iron front door, and a wolf that could swiftly clarify whether strangers were welcome in our yard at 2:00 in the morning.

Think carefully now that you have read my account. Close your eyes and imagine if we were doing this ministry in Somalia. It is not as confusing an issue as many seem to think. Things would be vastly different in our thinking if we would only allow ourselves to see ministry for what it is. God requires of each of us a faithfulness to ministry that does not limit *where* it takes place. My brother's death constantly reminds me that every person on the street matters. Not a single one of those gang members on the street was worth losing. Just because we are not aware of their deaths does not release us from the responsibility of doing something about it. Jesus has already died to save each one. Who is going to love them so that they too may have the chance for salvation and eternal life?

I think back on the many kids who are now off the street and living with Jesus. Many of them are attending church and bringing others to the Lord. Still others have gone to college and have entered career roles as well. I am satisfied that we did the right thing in persisting with gang ministry. Whenever I get the chance, I'm always back on the street to find them, one at a time. Indeed, we have not truly learned to live until we have found what we are willing to die for.

CHAPTER NINE

IT TAKES VISION

J ust as we were preparing to launch the new conference youth ministry initiative, the phone rang yet again. This time the call came from Maryland. To my surprise, my friend Ramona Perez Greek shared with me the fact that the youth director of the North American Division had taken a position in ADRA and that the division office was preparing to fill the vacancy. At first I thought she wanted suggestions for possible names. But I soon found out that she had discussed *my* name with North American Division administrators!

She had only one counsel to offer me as she completed her report of the process under way in the East. "Stay close to the Lord," she said. "You may need Him more than you've ever thought." As we concluded our discussion, Ramona led us in prayer. Her prayer, in its eloquent simplicity, asked God to make His will clear in the matter and give me peace. Then she left me to swallow hard and think of what might be happening in Maryland.

Ramona was the assistant director of women's ministries for the North American Division at the time. We had on many occasions discussed various issues of visioning in leadership. Also we had worked together on several projects for Latino youth and had participated in a camp meeting. I have a deep respect for Ramona. Like Pastor Benavides, she has been a wonderful mentor in the complex art of administration.

Ramona possesses a unique gift for seeing three steps ahead in a leadership process. Her keen understanding of human nature enables her to foresee developments in an administrative structure with both discipline and maturity. Whenever I have the opportunity I eagerly pick her brain. Because of her humble way, she probably doesn't even notice that I do it. Ramona is among those few leaders from whom I learn something every time I come into contact with her.

The news of the search for a new youth director at the North American Division made me soberly ponder its implications. The idea of my name even being considered at NAD was a great honor. However, I found out that there were 25 other names of highly qualified people already on the list. That kind of a fact can help a person keep a levelheaded perspective. For me it was more "the honor of being nominated." But I really didn't expect anything beyond that. So I did my best to put it out of my mind. At least I tried. I'm not sure I succeeded.

I saw Pastor Willie Oliver of New York at a youth event in Anaheim later that next weekend. I knew that NAD was also strongly considering him for the same youth ministries position. Willie told me that he had informed the NAD administration that he was not interested in the position at that time because of his new assignment working as youth director with David Taylor in the Atlantic Union. Then he turned to me and said that it was his impression that NAD was quite seriously considering my name. Feeling that familiar nausea in the pit of my stomach, I assured him that I didn't expect that to happen.

Later that next week my conference president, Herb Broekel, phoned to say that he had just heard from Alfred McClure, president of the North American Division. Herb soberly informed me that the NAD was going to extend to me a formal request to serve as the youth ministries director for North America. He asked me to clear my schedule and go home for the rest of the day and await the telephone call that evening. Before we hung up he advised, "Pray with Ruthie, José. The Lord will help you think clearly on this." I promised him I would do just that.

Ruthie and I literally spent the rest of the day talking and praying about the impending offer. We could not quite absorb the enormity of the challenge that lay before us. I contacted

Pastor Tony Anobile, another friend who shares my same passion for ministry. I asked for his counsel. Tony asked me pro and con questions about the offer, then also prayed with me, requesting God to lead.

I called Sergio and Chari in Miami. They felt that God could be behind the opportunity. Sergio prayed with me and gave me words of support and comfort. But I was amazed that I needed more comfort than support! Feelings of complete inadequacy can overpower you at such times. He told me that it was how you feel when you face a real challenge. If someone thinks that they are able to do everything God summons them to do, they will discover the hard way that that is not the case. I was about to learn how to depend on God as never before, Sergio explained.

Finally that evening McClure phoned. Nervously I told him that it was "not every day that the president of our church in North America calls me at home." After a few more pleasantries McClure got to the point. He officially offered the directorship of youth ministries for North America. I asked him to describe the territory to me. Pastor McClure explained that it consisted of 58 conferences and nine unions within the countries of Canada, the United States, and Bermuda. Teens and young adults numbered approximately 260,000 in more than 4,600 churches. The task was both massive and daunting.

Pastor McClure said that he had never in his career seen a selection process go as this one had. He stated his belief that the Lord was guiding and had brought us to this point. Also he said that the meeting of union presidents who had recommended my name had been "spirited" and included the strong participation of David Taylor. As we concluded the conversation I asked for time to pray with Ruthie. Pastor McClure understood and agreed to give us a little time.

I called Broekel and assured him that we would go to Washington to see the job description and the housing situation with an open mind. Ruthie and I would pray and ask God to show us what we should do. I was not going to rush into it. To be truthful, I must say, I was actually terrified.

Next I phoned Pastor Benavides and Ernie Castillo, the secretary of the Pacific Union, and asked their views and counsel. After some weighing of the options, each took time to pray with me. Then I contacted Tony Anobile again as we now considered the serious potential of going to Maryland. I trust Tony's instincts, and he did not disappoint me. As he had done earlier in the day, he prayed with me again.

Monte Sahlin—"Make things happen . . ."

Ruthie and I flew out to the Washington, D.C., area for the first time in our lives on a January day in 1994. When we arrived I felt intimidated by the Adventist world headquarters building that also housed the North American Division offices. It was snowing lightly outside, and the cold penetrated our thin California clothing. What did we know about dressing for snow? But as we got out of the car I wasn't sure if I trembled more from fear than the cold.

We met with Monte Sahlin, who served as assistant to the NAD president at the time. Monte was someone I had watched for several years. As a division leader for adult ministries, he had made an indelible mark on the church through the way he dealt with complex church issues. When I had sat with him on a committee a year earlier, his handling of some of the challenges that we were trying to address had astounded me.

To begin with, Monte sees all issues in light of how they will eventually make a difference at the local church. Whether it be an administrative issue, a product, or service item, he would make a committee work until they came up with the measurable results needed by the leaders who make ministry happen each week in congregations across the land. I had come to regard Monte as one of the foremost activist leaders in Adventism. He had clear objectives for both community and leadership. And he did it in a context that made sense to me as a pastor and conference official.

When Ruthie and I talked with him about the youth ministries position, I naturally felt hesitant. I knew that working with him would mean that my assignment would have to be measurable in local ministry terms. I also knew that the division hoped that the Lord would help us develop a new youth structure that would unleash the spiritual and physical energy of the thousands of young people in churches and campuses across the continent.

The stakes were high, and I felt completely unprepared for

the new task. What I wanted to find out was what the division expected from my work. Watching him intently, I asked Monte what he personally saw as my new role. His answer, as always, was simple. "Take the good ideas that you develop with your planning committee and then make them happen," he said. He pointed out that too often leaders produce ideas that go nowhere. The church's greatest need is for people "who make things happen."

After prayer with Monte, we agreed that Ruthie and I would give him an answer in two days. Then I had a brief meeting with Ted Wick, the previous NAD youth director. Ted shared with me the challenges and the victories of the previous six years of his tenure, and made a point of telling me that he felt that God had brought me there. He said that he had confidence that the Lord would use me in this capacity and encouraged me to accept the offer. It moved me that my immediate predecessor would express such firm support.

When Ruthie and I left the building that afternoon we returned to our hotel room across the street from the General Conference. As we watched the snow falling softly outside, we wondered what our next step should be. For the first time in our ministry, we decided that we would set out a "fleece" before the Lord as Gideon had done in the Bible.

That afternoon we prayed in that hotel room and laid before the Lord a challenge for two specific things. First, we needed a house. Housing in the Washington, D.C., area is a nightmare for most Californians. The cost of housing is so high that we knew that others had turned down jobs simply because they could not afford to live there. Second, we needed financing for the house. Because the crimes we were still suffering in Fresno had hurt us financially, we did not know who would loan us money in the area.

We looked at various housing possibilities and came away with the usual assortment of "we can't afford that" experiences. That night, a Dr. Dysinger, whom we had never met, stopped by our hotel room and said, "I have your house!" Later he took us to see a home in a development called Pitcairn Place. It consisted of large townhouses surrounded by a wooded area. Originally built for General Conference leaders in the past, it had a crime-free record during its 23-year history. We liked the house immediately.

The next day we questioned several leaders about financing options in the area. The same day we secured commitments for financing the house! Ruthie and I were in shock. Perhaps the fleece should have been a more difficult one. We knelt again in our hotel room, and as we prayed, we knew deep inside that God was calling a Western family to move to the East. The next day, as promised, I went in to see Monte and formally accepted.

I swallowed several times as I stood there. He could see that I was afraid. In his customary way, Monte stood and stretched out his hand. As we shook hands, he said, "Welcome to the North American Division. Don't worry, you'll do all right. You're surrounded by some very talented people who will work closely with you."

Taking a deep breath, I asked, "Will you help me?"

Monte smiled, "Of course I will; that's why I'm here—to see that you and the other directors succeed."

Over the next three months we moved from Fresno to Maryland, where our home was only five miles from the office. Everything was new—woods instead of the forests, hills instead of the mountains, and winding roads instead of straight streets. What was most refreshing was the absence of gunfire at night. No more crime and terror at 2:00 in the morning. The gangs in Fresno had stolen each of my vehicles seven times, so they arrived with lots of damage. I would spend the next five years working to keep them running.

I walked into my new role with great hesitation, realizing that in leadership you cannot possibly please everyone, a rule that applies even from the very beginning. I had not known what it was like to work with a network of more than 900 youth ministry specialists. It definitely makes you understand issues from a larger perspective. Just as there are Democrats and Republicans in the politics of Washington, D.C., so there are also different and dedicated points of view in ministry. The massive variations in cultures, races, and languages in North America made it inevitable that I would face a diverse and complicated task, guaranteeing many differences in opinion.

My first meetings with national and international youth leaders were difficult, with occasional tense moments when such differences came to the surface. I knew that these tensions reflected what many of our churches face. The Lord made it clear that if I was going to accomplish anything, I was going to have to spend more time on my knees. Each meeting and planning session made it obvious that we could not possibly resolve the problems faced by our youth. The answer could not be found in human wisdom. We would have to learn to rely on the Lord to accomplish the impossible. God is the one who wants to do the impossible things. And the beauty is that He wants to do them *through* us.

As God does His work through his people, we must leave no room for confusion about whose wisdom is leading. Why anyone can ever crave international leadership also puzzles me. There is neither glamour nor glory in the stress of this kind of leadership. Not even those few moments when crowds express support and admiration can make such leadership easy.

The flip side of that same experience is the fact that you are always under scrutiny. People can easily identify a leader's humanity. What you learn to pray for, is the day when they recognize God in His work. Although building consensus becomes the task of a lifetime, only the Lord can move planning forward. Each committee must confirm through their actions that God alone is best suited to lead His own ministry.

Alfred McClure—Take risks for mission . . .

As we worked to develop a premise and structure for teen and young adult ministries in North America, I always made it a point to consult with our president, Al McClure. Whenever I had a new chart or diagram for the next level of the process, I would check with him so that he would be informed and could also provide input. Pastor McClure takes deep interest in what our youth can do in our churches. His questions are always searching and detailed.

One day I asked him what strengths he perceived in our developing plan for our young people. Glancing up from the chart on the table in front of him, he said, "I see that your team is working to take the many gifts that youth possess and focus them on mission." Then he reflected on how he had looked forward to the "army of youth" materializing in our church since his earliest years in ministry. He shared with me that he was highly committed to mobilizing young people and encouraging our churches to empower their youth. Years earlier McClure had helped a group of young adults in an NAD Youth Evangelism Task Force study the issue of outreach and bring recommendations to the denomination. My work was a response to those recommendations.

With a sigh Pastor McClure expressed his personal concern over how much time our church argues over issues ranging from theology to church policy. He did not see the issues themselves as unimportant, because some have to be dealt with. Rather, his concern was more fundamental. He felt that when our churches divert vital energy to long-term arguments, we often lose sight of mission. I could see the sadness in his eyes. With that thought in mind, he asked me to do all I could to avoid unnecessary divisions and arguments, and keep the focus of youth ministry on outreach.

McClure then challenged me not to "divert our focus from mission, no matter what comes up along the way." I assured him that I too agreed with his vision of focusing only on our reason for existence. "Never be afraid to take risks for mission," he urged. Although he knew that we sought to expand the role of youthful gifts in churches and schools, he also recognized the formidable difficulties we would face. His comments reflected the deep commitment he has for our youth. By challenging me to take risks, he was signaling his own willingness to take them also.

I recognized that another of those special moments was occurring in my life. Realizing how much the president of our denomination in North America was prepared to support our young people in new and empowering ways, I leaned forward and said, "The Lord will move our young people in outreach." Pastor McClure then led us in prayer. As I walked out of his office, he hugged me, saying, "The Lord is going to do great things." I knew that I had made a covenant for our young people before the Lord. While I still felt afraid, I sensed that God was going before us. That gave me a special peace.

My schedule immediately included lots of travel and an intensive schedule of meetings. I met with student leaders and conference and union administrators. As the purpose of youth and young adult ministries came into focus during my second year in our planning committees and advisories, we launched into the new structure. After the vote of the year-end meetings in Battle Creek, we announced that the purpose of youth ministries in North America is outreach. In a document entitled "Saved to Serve" we inaugurated seven initiatives that we hoped would build a vision for the empowerment of local youth ministry in the churches of North America.

Later that year we initiated the Adventist Youth Service Network, or YouthNet. The Student Missions program, Taskforce, Young Pioneers, Native Messengers, and other mission opportunities give young people the chance to dedicate a year of their lives in service for Christ. We asked God to help us model for the churches of the division a process in which young people can be trusted with real leadership.

One day Pastor McClure and I traveled together to participate in a Global Mission rally entitled "Hands Across the World." Several thousand people attended the event in Atlanta. I was scheduled to be on the platform with him and other General Conference leaders. Just before we lined up backstage I asked McClure if I could speak with him. We walked over to a nearby corner.

Since I was going to preach in the meeting, unveiling some of the new directions and initiatives for our youth, I asked him if he had any counsel for me. "Tell them the vision of what the Lord has called our youth to do," he said. I bowed my head. I knew that the moment had come to develop a new chapter in North American teen and young adult ministries. As I stood there I felt that familiar nausea of hesitation.

"Chief, I feel scared," I said softly.

Leaning over, he whispered into my ear, "I'm scared too. Let's go do this." The Lord moved mightily in that meeting.

That year we brought a young adult, Byard Parks, to the division office to serve as a student missionary in a role that gave him the authority to assist us in structuring and launching YouthNet. Celeste Ryan, another young adult already at the division office when I arrived, made *Adventist View* magazine a growing influence across the land. We later added other young adults with specific assignments for the NAD. One young adult who has also served with distinction is Allan Martin. He has helped put all NAD youth ministries on-line, both on CompuServe and the Internet, as well as directed various other programs and events with youth professionals.

This phase of the new launch was vital. We were attempting to model in the General Conference building what we are asking of the churches. The reason for this is that people cannot always be persuaded to think in new ways about youth at a church board or when reading an article. But when they see actual examples of a new way of thinking, they can realize that young people can actually lead when given the opportunity.

Our initiatives for young people in North America are premised on this principle. We therefore need more and more churches to demonstrate what young people can do to influence the congregation and the world for Christ. In so doing, youth will prove that it matters not whether people are young or old, whether they are experienced or inexperienced, but whether they are filled with the Holy Spirit.

Ruthie Jacobsen—"A prayer movement"

As ministry progressed, we saw miracle after miracle occurring among our youth across North America. One of the most significant developments of the late 1980s and the early 1990s was the growth of the prayer movement among the people. From time to time periodical articles would tell of powerful incidents of prayer in ministry, but soon such reports blossomed into a growing movement for prayer conferences in many places.

For years my wife, Ruthie, and I have prayed about everything in our lives, because we believe in the unmistakable power of prayer. We had experienced miracles before and saw each step of our ministerial life permeated by the blessing of prayer. When I first heard of the prayer conference movement, however, I didn't really think too much about it.

But this prayer movement was vastly different. Sometimes in life we encounter something that we cannot explain in words. Have you ever tried to describe to another person what it is like to stand at Yosemite Valley, the Grand Canyon, or Niagara Falls? If you are a parent, have you ever attempted to tell someone who has no children what having your own means to you? In like manner, I could not possibly know what a prayer conference was from just reading the reports.

The leader of the prayer movement, selected by the North American Division, is Ruthie Jacobsen. Ever since she had served in the Oregon Conference where her husband, Don, was the president, I heard accounts of the ministry's rapid growth. The day came when Ruthie and a team of youth pastors—Gary Burns, Gary Parks, and Peter Nieri—approached me about attending a prayer conference. It would be a teen prayer conference in Gentry, Arkansas, and they wanted me to speak to the young people gathered there. I agreed to go without any idea of what I was about to experience.

When I arrived at the academy for the event, I found more than 400 teenagers involved in small group Bible studies—throughout the auditorium, in hallways, in rooms, and even outside. Breakaway groups would also frequently gather for prayer. As I would listen to their prayers I found that they were praying for each other, or for kids that were struggling with some problem. I had never seen such intensity. The youth were completely immersed in what was happening. This was *not* a youth congress . . . it was a miracle.

When we gathered for the plenary sessions in the auditorium, the youth sang with the gusto of a celebration. The worship was overwhelmingly spiritual. They read scriptures continuously between songs, with testimonies interspersed throughout the program. The next night during the plenary session the youth were even more animated because they had gone out into the community to minister for the Lord.

What struck me also was the large variety of ministries that they carried out. Some went out to distribute magabooks, others led Bible studies, some cleaned highways, and still others volunteered at a homeless shelter in Tulsa, Oklahoma. The variety pointed to the commitment Ruthie Jacobsen and the prayer ministries team had made to uphold all gifts as legitimate and important for God's work. This element is critical to understanding today's approach for ministry. We need all gifts at the front lines of the ministry battlefield.

Each night at the plenary session the students could not stop testifying. Testimonies continued for more than two hours. When the preacher finally got up to speak, suddenly a student interrupted him, declaring that he knew what had just been said was true, because he had himself had experienced it that day on the street. Another young person added her testimony to that report. Still others stood and testified about how their experiences confirmed the sermon also. After a while, the preacher, realizing that the students had taken over the meeting, sat down and marveled at what the Lord was doing in the lives of these youth . . . and more important, what the Lord was doing in the life of the community with these youth!

Ruthie Jacobsen and the prayer team youth pastors gathered around me the next day and asked how I felt about the conference. I could sense that they had been praying about that moment with me for some time. As I nodded my head, I could only say that, had I not seen it with my own eyes and heard with my own ears, I could have never fully understood the power of this ministry.

Clearly prayer ministry is not any kind of secret weapon. Yet it is a weapon that we overlook more often than we realize! My wife and I have for years relied on prayer throughout each day. But this experience took me giant leaps forward in understanding the untapped power of the prayer relationship with God. Prayer ministry showed me that a greater intimacy can develop between God and His people with each passing day of fellowship with Him.

The effect on a person's ability to minister is overwhelming too. The enhanced vision for the role of prayer that Ruthie Jacobsen and her team taught me, clarified the single, most critical element we needed to move the youth and young adult ministry plan forward. Prayer is the key. It goes far beyond the prayers involved in planning and mobilizing ministry. Young people themselves need to be brought face-to-face with God through the door that prayer will open for them. The prayer conference is a corporate experience that takes young people to a personal relationship of prayer and Bible study—and that leads to a lifestyle of ministry with the Lord.

Unlimited power resides in such prayer relationships. If our young people are to become the kind of warriors that God has promised us, it will not be because we have merely given them good tools and training. It is because God Himself equips youth with His grace and the power of His Spirit. Only then will they become a threat to the powers of darkness. Prayer is the key.

I have knelt many times with Ruthie Jacobsen and her team of youth pastors, forming a bond of mutual commitment. All of us are determined to see the Lord advance His will through the power of prayer in the lives of His people. We have prayed many times over victories and challenges alike. Our conviction of prayer's vital role only grows by the day. My own prayer life has seen a wonderful increase in blessing.

As the "Saved to Serve" initiatives unfolded around the division, and youth continued to respond to the challenges of the ministry, we could not be prepared for the enormity of what God would do. Soon we worked with Randy Wisbey to establish a Center for Youth Evangelism at Andrews University. It focused on empowering youth through developing a curriculum that consisted of seven principles for local church youth ministry. Pastor Ron Whitehead, the associate director for teen and young adult ministries for the North American Division, now leads a team of 22 young people. There they develop materials, services, products, and many other tools and experiences in ministry.

The greatest result of what God is doing appears in the leadership of the young people themselves. For several years young people have coordinated an event called "Go." From 200 to 400 young people come together to talk about, pray about, and plan about, mission! An incredible spirit of faith and boldness leads many young people to volunteer a year of their lives to serve as missionaries. Their testimonies confirm how the Lord leads dramatically in the lives of these youthful leaders as they serve. This event is about to grow dramatically.

Another phenomenal ministry comes out of the Center for Youth Evangelism. Entitled the "YouthNet eXtreme" team, this group of four young adults travels throughout North America in a truck, pulling a fully equipped trailer that allows them to minister in churches, schools, camp meetings, and elsewhere. They show their peers that something is happening that goes far beyond a mere program. It leads to incredible decisions for Christ. On their first outing at the Mountain View Camp meeting in West Virginia in 1998, 11 people gave their lives to the Lord in baptism!

In Houston, Texas, an organization called "Young Adult System" (YAS) launched a ministry to make a difference in both the lives of their peers and the community. The young people select projects in the city to bring people together in ministry. In Dallas a similar ministry seeks to locate young adults who have not attended church for a while. Berkeley, California, has a group of students at the university that formed another ministry. It reaches out to other students and forms bonds with Pacific Union College and additional ministry locations. Still other public campus ministries in the Carolinas, in Florida, Tennessee, Los Angeles, Massachusetts, and many other places have young people leading their peers in the Lord.

In August of 1998 an event called "eXcite '98" took place at La Sierra University. Two young adults, Shasta Burr and Jennifer Tyner, led a team of young adults in challenging their peers to jump into the fray of ministry and reach new heights for the Lord. As a follow-up, it had an event at the General Conference headquarters called "conneXions '99." As young people embraced more ministry objectives, they even raised money to help fund the many projects.

Coinciding with that event was another named "Access '99." In it young adults on the campuses of the Adventist colleges of North America also committed to ministry. Held at Walla Walla College, it was beamed by satellite across the continent. Many young people made commitments in a large variety of ministry goals. Additional events and organizations have come together in the past few years with the same objectives to mobilize for ministry.

Student missionaries are going out across the globe in larger numbers. New and innovative ministries for social action are continuing to blossom as well, as exhibited by the success of the Stahl Center at La Sierra University. Community ministries are on the increase, with most Adventist college and university campuses reporting large numbers of students actively making a difference in their towns. The Hancock Center for Youth and Family Ministry also mobilizes students in ministry projects and the development of products for use in ministry.

The Lord has taken the ministry far beyond what we ever imagined would occur when the effort began. For many years, wonderful leaders have led our young people in countless successful ministries. We have seen how the Lord provided the fertile soil and sowed the blessing. These seeds led to further planning of a youth ministry structure, and finally, to the launch of specific initiatives that would further expand the movement among young people. But I must say again that this is not what has caused such ministry to grow so rapidly. Each day confirms even further that no human plans can even begin to do the ministry that needs to happen. Only God can do His work. And only He can do the impossible results that He has promised.

Here is where the miracle of prayer ministry bore fruit. When the young people of our church began to gather to pray, search God's word, and make commitments, the Lord took them forward from there. The most decisive movements in history have been those directed by God. By their fruits we have recognized them. Perhaps the most significant fruit we have seen in most of these events and ministries has been the strong conviction of our young people to "stop being angry with our church."

This generation of young people is beginning to demonstrate that they are filled with the Holy Spirit. By laying at the feet of Jesus their pain for the many wrongs they have suffered over the years, a growing number of our young people are sounding a new call for reconciliation. There is an open willingness to forgive and dialogue. It is time for young and old to come together as never before. Imagine a ministry, powered by the Spirit, filled with talented adults, and driven by the limitless energy and gifts that can only come from young people! Can it be that an "army" is at last rising among us?

CHAPTER TEN

A POLICY
OF OUTREACH

The rapidly growing youth ministry across the division has increased and changed the demands of leadership. One of the realities of leadership today is that, in many ways, it may never again be what it was like in the past. One fundamental difference involves the impact of technology. Too many leaders underestimate this aspect, because for many of us, technology is "new."

Some just want to use technology to enhance and improve our traditional models of leadership. But today's youth rarely think in the old patterns. Many of us regard a computer as a wonderful invention to make things smoother, quieter, and more efficient. But our youth view the computer as the gateway to vast regions of space to explore and incorporate into our daily lives. As theorized by Einstein's theory of relativity, they enter technology for a short time and return transformed in ways we cannot identify by traditional terms.

We must bear in mind that the so-called Generation X has been immersed in technology most of their lives. Because of that experience, the generation often prides itself in how different it is from all previous ones. This generation perceives the world very differently from their parents. Consequently, we cannot be surprised that the task of joining forces with them is challenging. Most of this generation is now in their 20s.

But all of us, including the so-called Gen Xers, are in for a rude awakening. The newest generation is already surfacing among us. This virtual subculture, the millennials, was symbolically born with wires in their ears. Most of it does not know when AIDS began, for example, because the disease has been around all of their lives. They have seen sonograms of themselves in their mother's bodies. In many cases they even have videos of their births. Calculators that we bought for $200 they buy for $1 at the Dollar Store. Many millennials have never even seen a record player!

The computer chip has changed the face of the planet we live on. We feel triumphant if we take the latest WordPerfect upgrade course. This generation often writes their own software. Some of us brag about learning how to "surf the Web." Millennials develop their own websites. Many of the millennial generation have had advanced computers in their school classrooms since the day they entered kindergarten. There is no way even to begin to explain the extent to which this current generation has left many of us behind, both in the perception and the development of the future that they will dominate.

The computer chip is a two-edged sword. That which was invented for our blessing can also be the greatest curse. We could easily argue that the computer chip is the modern version of the tree of the knowledge of good and evil. Our dilemma is that this tree is now available at a younger and younger age. What my daughter knows today at age 11, I didn't learn until I was 17. Some of us may panic when we see just how much our children have discovered about technology's impact for evil. But we must also remember that the same child, filled with the Holy Spirit, will use that technology to help take the gospel to the entire world! Our society therefore faces a challenge that we can not ignore or take lightly.

As we prayed about these challenges, we discussed on numerous occasions the kinds of mindsets necessary to continue building leadership structures for youth. In other words, we are finding that it is not our role to resist the culture that God promised us would come. Although we see people "running to and fro," and knowledge has "increased," merely to condemn the current generation is to miss the joy of what God promised. I would suggest that we need leadership that not only understands this reality, but also moves aggressively to focus it. Rather than fighting to control young people, it appears that God wants us to channel their boundless energy into a vision of leadership in local church ministries.

Leadership structures, therefore, need to move from predominantly bureaucratic patterns to more activist forms of operation. To counter a technological world, we need more human contact with the divine than ever before. That, I believe, is why we see the growing prayer phenomenon among God's people. The Lord is intervening, taking the raw energy that youth possess and focusing it for His glory.

Young people tell us we need more policies that encourage and support them doing things in ministry, rather than policies that simply preserve current systems and rules. If we shift to a more activist leadership, then we must always be formulating initiatives that will model ministry opportunities for our youth. In this way we can encourage churches to do likewise. The most logical place to develop more opportunities for youth to serve in ministry leadership is in local congregations and the communities that surround them.

The sobering reality of the challenge that we as leaders faced drove us back to our knees to ask the Lord to provide ways for our denomination to exert more influence in the community. Seeking more opportunities for young people to serve, we began to identify the humanitarian assets the church already possessed. For example, through the Adventist Community Services we have an agreement with the Red Cross and the Federal Emergency Management Agency that designates us official goods-distribution specialists for most American natural disasters. Our church also operates one of the largest Protestant school systems in the country. And our Adventist hospital system has a prestigious reputation.

With just these huge advantages, we knew that it was indeed possible for the Adventist Church to become a major humanitarian leader in the United States. The key would be on how effectively we could get our work recognized and consulted by other national leaders, including those in government. I discussed several ideas with Monte Sahlin. As the executive director of Adventist Community Services at that time, he joined us in the growing burden. We concluded that enlarging the visibility of Adventism's humanitarian projects would be a wonderful foundation for a larger evangelistic strategy for our church.

With all of the many grassroots movements of young people sprouting up around the world, this development would provide further infrastructure for young people to expand ministries with their churches. It soon became obvious, though, that we would need to carefully maintain clear distinctions between partisan political issues and humanitarian leadership.

The moment arrived for us to move forward. One day I received an invitation to a congressional banquet for Latino leaders. My wife and I prayed about it and also consulted with Ruthie Jacobsen and the prayer team. After prayer and counsel at her house I went home to my wife, and together we decided we would attend the banquet. The event was a black-tie affair unlike anything I had ever been a part of before. As we entered the banquet room, I turned to my Ruthie and said, "Let's see what the Lord has for us to do tonight."

The meal was elegant. I had never sat at a table where the setting included a knife, three forks, two spoons, etc. What I needed most was a warm stack of tortillas, and then I would have been fine. During the program various prominent speakers addressed the audience on Latino issues in the country. Then the keynote speaker for the evening walked out to the platform: the president of the United States.

As the president spoke, I asked the Lord what it was He wanted us to do that night. I had watched the program carefully and noticed the difference between congressional and presidential protocol. For the first time in my life I became more aware of governmental institutions. Until then I had tended to see government from the perspective of a political party or interest group. But that night it became very clear that, as in the time of Joseph and Daniel, government is more than the politics that surrounds it.

At a certain point in his speech, the president referred to the various programs across the country for tutoring children in reading. At that moment I turned to my wife and said, "Ruthie, that's why we're here." When she asked what I meant, I told her that YouthNet was currently launching tutoring sites with Adventist Community Services around the United States and we could provide leadership to others in the effort. Tutoring underprivileged children with their reading skills could be a wonderful expression of who we are as a church. It would also generate more sites for young people to serve the community in God's name.

As the president finished his presentation, he walked down onto the main floor and began to greet the guests. Ruthie took my hand and said, "Let's go meet the president." Before we knew it, we were standing with him and shaking hands. I told him of the tutoring sites that we were launching and that we would be happy to help others in their efforts. The president responded with a hug and encouraged me to move ahead with the tutoring.

As we left the banquet room, two close friends, Carlos and Iris Sibrian, joined us. Iris is a television reporter in Washington, D.C., and was the one who had contacted the congressional group about inviting me. She had found my name in their database. As the four of us went outside, we talked briefly about what had just happened and decided that we needed to go to the Lord about what He wanted us to do in the future. As other guests filed out of the ballroom, the four of us gathered in a little circle to pray.

I felt a certain sick feeling again in the pit of my stomach—that familiar nausea that comes when the Lord introduces me to something entirely new. As each of us prayed, we asked the Lord to show us what He wanted to happen. We needed to know if there was a difference between a memorable meal and a new opportunity to minister in evangelism.

As we concluded our prayers, we noticed that we were standing where President Reagan had been shot 16 years earlier. As we bade each other good night, Iris turned to me and said, "I've worked in this city for many years, and I don't know why, but I believe you're going to see the president again." I walked away with a deep sense of confusion. What contact would a youth and volunteerism director ever have with the president of the United States? I was afraid to think too much about it. The most difficult element on my mind at that point was the knowledge that President Clinton was not popular among many of our people.

The very next day I received a phone call from Iris. She told me Suzana Valdez, who served at the White House as an assistant to the president, was waiting to hear from me. Iris gave me the number and said that Suzana wanted to discuss our tutoring initiative. Immediately I went to see Monte Sahlin, and we put in writing the initiative for our youth to tutor children in reading. The idea was that our denomination would take a leadership role in serving the community and hopefully inspire other organizations. In so doing, we could create an image that would portray Christ in new ways to people never before exposed to Adventism.

I then went to see Dr. Clarence Hodges, public affairs and religious liberty director for NAD. Clarence had served as children's commissioner and assistant secretary of state under President Ronald Reagan. I needed his views and counsel regarding the new opportunity. When he asked me what I wanted to do, I said that I wanted to give the tutoring proposal to the White House and then see how we could also link it to other national organizations as a testimony to what the Adventist Church is doing to benefit humanity. Clarence agreed to the wisdom of the plan and gave his approval.

After leaving the document at the White House with Suzana, I returned to the office and discussed the details with Monte. We put it in the Lord's hands and moved on with our many other priorities. My travel and committee schedule was so full that I had no more time to even think about the new development. After a few weeks I pushed the proposal to the back of my mind.

Some months later the president joined General Colin Powell in announcing a presidential summit for volunteerism in Philadelphia the next April. I remembered that our tutoring proposal was already at the White House. Through some help from a friend, we secured an appointment at General Powell's office to leave a copy of the proposal with them since the General was working with the White House as chairman of the event. After a few visits with members of Congress we received enough endorsements Adventist Community Services received two seats at the summit.

Former presidents, key national leaders, 36 governors, 100 mayors, and a few hundred other guests attended the event. Both former Republican and Democratic presidents sounded a common call for America to serve those in need and provide a future for our children. We were a part of a national summons to community action. What made that moment special was the fact that our Adventist efforts have been bearing fruit for many decades. The quantity and quality of service that our people give in the Lord's name had positioned our ministry for leadership.

Flo McAfee—A policy of outreach . . .

Some time before the summit, Clarence Hodges gave me the name of an assistant to the president named Flo McAfee. As I dialogued with her, I found that she was the point person for the president's involvement at the event. She and I had many conversations by phone as the summit drew near. At one point the White House even considered placing me on a discussion panel.

Flo made sure that we received ample opportunities to participate in the discussions among the many leaders who would be present at the summit. Both Monte and I officially participated as national invitees to what was formally titled the Presidents' Summit for America's Future. When I arrived that April 1997 morning at the opening ceremonies in front of Liberty Hall in Philadelphia, I looked for my seating area according to a color-coded card I had received. To my surprise, my card indicated that I would be in the White House Staff section at the front. I looked around, but could not see Flo. She had given me a choice seat, and I began to see the kind of person that she is.

As the summit activities progressed, General Colin Powell did a wonderful job of chairing, taking us through the various challenges faced by America's youth. The speakers presented a dramatic display of united concern for the country's children and the immediate need for us to actually get involved in meeting them. Former presidents George Bush, Gerald Ford, and Jimmy Carter were accompanied by Nancy Reagan, who represented her husband. All spoke to the goals being laid out by the various organizations at the summit.

As I looked in the booklet listing the organizations making a difference and meeting the nation's challenges, I was moved to see Adventist Community Services listed with our goal of launching 100 tutoring sites in 10 cities around the U.S. As of this writing we now have more than half of them in operation and expect the rest before the end of the year.

After the summit I thanked Flo for the privilege of being involved, and she graciously thanked us for our own commitment to the effort. There was something very different about her. We remained in contact, and eventually we developed a friendship that I have come to treasure. Flo McAfee is an unassuming leader that makes critically important things happen in the most humble of ways. Soon, as I got to know her better, I found that she is a devoted and loving Christian who will literally give her sweater away if someone needs it.

As I worked with her to enhance our efforts for communities across the country, I learned from her vast experience. She always took time to explain to me the implications of a situation and the principles involved in a particular decision process. When I asked her to summarize what she does, Flo responded simply, "It's a policy of outreach." I thought about that for a long time afterward. As a church we have sought to develop policies of outreach with varying levels of success. But Flo *lives* a policy of outreach in her daily experience with people.

A short time later she left full-time service as the assistant to the president. The president himself felt her absence, because she had been a pivotal leader on his staff. One of her greatest assets is her ability to bring people together on community goals. Another of her gifts is her skill in managing key events and initiatives. For example, she coordinated the meetings during the Israeli-Palestinian peace talks that led to the historic handshake between Yasir Arafat and Yitzhak Rabin on the South Lawn of the White House.

Thinking I had lost Flo's leadership, I grieved for a bit, but my pain quickly subsided. The White House continued to bring her in as a consultant to the president, and her role became even more influential. Flo had by then increased her involvement both with local community organizations as well as larger organizations such as the National Prostate Cancer Coalition, while still making major contributions by working directly with the president.

She powerfully demonstrated to me that the most effective leadership is not based on titles, but on measurable results in people's lives. Flo helps local organizations become effective in their community, while at the same time she assists the president of the United States to have a greater impact on everyday lives.

I wondered how someone could remain a humble servant while having so much authority and influence.

Over time, through her, I met other presidential staff and Cabinet secretaries with whom I worked to enlarge various humanitarian goals. During that same year we also established relationships with many congressional leaders of both parties on Capitol Hill. We spoke to legislation on volunteerism, disaster response, education, and other humanitarian priorities. To facilitate our work in Congress we even coleased an office for Adventist Community Services with the Washington Institute on Capitol Hill.

I began to send letters and memorandums to the president or the vice president, depending on the issue. It was during this time that I thought of Dr. Paul Landa at La Sierra University. When I sat in his classroom years earlier, he had stated that "only perfect work" was acceptable. The written paper on which most of the grade depended was the single most difficult class assignment of my life. Although at the time I had wondered about the value of such a course, I now understood why I had learned those skills in his classroom. When you send a six-page memorandum to the president of the United States, only perfect work is acceptable. I phoned Dr. Landa one day and deeply thanked him for his decisive contribution to my life.

In the succeeding years our work with the government has matured and remained focused. Whether I attend a briefing at the White House or Congress, or a ceremony as a guest, my role has remained the same. When I have worked with governmental leaders, it has been for the purpose of building coalitions across the country that can enlarge our ability to serve more people. Flo helped me to learn to focus leadership in a way that goes far beyond the partisanship that erects barriers between people in Washington, D.C. I realized that no matter who is in the White House, our denomination can still serve humanity.

As a result, many in government have gained a positive perception of Adventism. We are now increasingly being recognized as a humanitarian church that shares a Christ that cares for people and their needs. Always we need to remember that Jesus, the most powerful preacher of all time, was not known for His mouth, but for His hands. After He had used His hands to heal, bless, or raise someone from the dead, the thankful person would ask who He was. It was then that Jesus would open to that individual the powerful gospel of the kingdom of heaven. If people see what we as Adventists do with our hands to serve others in the name of Christ, they may be more willing to ask who we are. We will then have earned more authority to answer them with the gospel.

One day I invited Flo to go to La Sierra University and personally inspect the work that our young people are doing in their communities. The university was celebrating a week of service ministry, and she eagerly accepted. President Clinton later asked her to set up his meetings for his trip to South America, but she told him that she was already committed to us that week. It touched me that she would give us that kind of priority. When she visited the campus, she addressed the students and met many of the leaders from Riverside who coordinate various programs with us.

Afterward I took her to East Los Angeles, where we examined the city's needs. I then showed her what Adventist churches are doing to meet those needs. We stopped at one of the churches where a team of students and adult leaders briefed us on our on-going tutoring initiative in the city. Impressed, she returned the next Sabbath and met personally with the youth who tutored the children. Once again she demonstrated her capacity to work humbly and lovingly with local people on the very front lines where leadership matters most. During that visit she stood reverently and compassionately with me when we visited the place where my brother's body had been found.

That night we ate supper with Kelo and Sandra Suarez in Glendale, friends who opened their home for the occasion. Located on the Glendale hills, their home offers a dramatic view of the city, especially at night. We had a wonderful time of fun, laughter, and reflection. When we finished eating, we turned down the house lights so that we could see the lights outside. As we looked out the window, we joined in prayer together. Each of us prayed, reflecting our gratitude to God for the blessings of being able to serve humanity in the name of Christ.

My contacts with Flo opened up to me many new perspectives of national leadership that have been invaluable to me in our teen and young adult ministry. But I learned far more than that from her. She demonstrated to me her deepest foundations for leadership: servanthood, humility, and courage. When it comes time to act, she is unafraid, and absolutely committed. Her loyalty is profound and unwavering. This African-American woman has been invested with great authority, but she is content to be the activist leader who works quietly out of the public limelight. In so doing, she has powerfully shaped my own leadership skills.

Luis Trejo Rojas—Learn to live, "mijo" . . .

Believing that every experience God has allowed to happen to me has a purpose, I have sought to learn from every turn in life. Some think that learning slows down with age, but I disagree. Learning must increase as we get older, because the world is changing faster than ever before. We can grow along each step of life's path. But to stop growing is to stop leading.

As I think back to the days of my childhood, I remember my dad and the trauma of his unresolved pain. I often wondered if things would ever get better. But because Jesus entered our home, things did change with time. My dad, Luis Trejo Rojas, became my close friend. Just as the Lord reached me, he also reached my father. Although it took time, my dad has grown to become a special presence in the family. His role in the community also increased. At times he has given as many as 60 Bible studies a week.

I call home at least once a week and share the latest with Dad and Mom. Throughout the years Dad had often told me, "Aprende a vivir, mijo" (Learn to live, my son). He and my mom finally worked through their situation at home and now need each other more than ever. Love is a special thing.

As they grew in their lives, they passed the blessing on to their children. I thank the Lord that they pushed me to attend college. The deep value of their reproof when they saw me drifting kept me on course. But most of all, my parents have always made it clear that they believe in me. I thank God that their own growth made them strong leaders. Accepting Jesus was the ground in which the seed of leadership germinated in them. I love my parents and want to continue growing the way they do.

Like my parents, all of my mentors in life have had the same Jesus in common. As each of them reflected the character of

Christ, I have learned. I could not mention everyone that has influenced my life, for there would not be enough pages to adequately describe those experiences. But I have sought to share in simple terms some of the profound ways that God uses people to bless others. My life is not different from any other. We all are the products of what God teaches us in the experiences of our lives.

I challenge you, youth and young adults, to listen to the counsel of your elders. Although the cultures may clash, older people have had the advantage of living longer, and their experiences can be a wonderful blessing if you allow yourself to listen and learn. At times you will need to be patient, because you may hear them speak in the language of a past culture. But listen intently and you will grow. Just because you think something is outdated does not mean that it is wrong.

I would also challenge my older friends to view this generation of youth and young adults with new eyes. Resist the temptation to condemn whatever you find different. Remember that what we don't understand is not always bad. What we may fear the most in a particular young person may actually be the very gift God has given him or her to accomplish His will with. Take quality time for a young person. If people would not have taken time for me, I most likely would not be alive today. Many patient, longsuffering adults sacrificed to invest in my life, and I will be forever grateful. You hold the authority to freely give to a younger individual that which you have learned in life. But let them wear "their own armor" as you mentor them with prayer and counsel.

The Lord has a plan for all our lives. If we are faithful to His word, and listen to the counsel of those He sends along our way, we cannot possibly imagine all that God has in store for us. I have found that when I freely receive from the Lord, He expects me to faithfully give to others. This is leadership.

Technology may indeed be radically changing the world. But we know, through the Bible, that it will happen. So we must not be surprised. Inspiration has also told us that the "last movements shall be rapid ones." The time for us to make a bigger difference for others in our communities and around the world is now. All of this is impossible to accomplish on our own. Only God can do it. It is now incumbent upon all of us to allow Him to do these great things in ministry through our simple lives.

We must pray together as never before. We must commune with God in His Word. We must actively forgive each other our offenses. We must together ask for the outpouring of the Holy Spirit. In the final analysis, the most powerful leadership on earth is the result of the movement of the Holy Spirit—that which God does through the life of a humble, courageous, servant of people.